GRAND CANYON
a different view

CONTRIBUTIONS BY:

Steve Austin
John Baumgardner
Ken Cumming
Duane Gish
Werner Gitt
Ken Ham
Bill Hoesch
Russ Humphreys
Alex Lalomov
John MacArthur
Henry Morris
John Morris
Terry Mortenson
Mike Oard
Gary Parker
Scott Rugg
Andrew Snelling
Keith Swenson
Larry Vardiman
Tas Walker
John Whitcomb
Carl Wieland
Kurt Wise

Written and compiled by TOM VAIL

Chief photographer, CHARLY HEAVENRICH

Master Books

See to it that no one takes you captive through philosophy and empty deception, according to the tradition of men, according to the elementary principles of the world, rather than according to Christ. – Colossians 2:8

GRAND CANYON
a different view

First Printing: May 2003

Eighth Printing: June 2010

Printed in China

Cover and interior design by Brent Spurlock and Tom Vail

Please visit our web site for other great titles:
www.masterbooks.net

ISBN 13: 978-0-89051-373-6
ISBN 10: 0-89051-373-2

Library of Congress Catalog Number: 2002116471

All photography by Charly Heavenrich unless otherwise noted

Cover Photo: "Morning Fog in Marble Canyon" by Charly Heavenrich

All illustrations by Bryan Miller

All contributions have been peer-reviewed to ensure a consistent and biblical perspective.

All Scripture is from the New American Standard Bible.

Back cover image (center) — Marble Canyon
(Courtesy of Arizona River Runners)

TABLE OF CONTENTS

INTRODUCTION

The Grand Canyon of the Colorado is recognized as one of the greatest wonders of the natural world, breathtaking in its incredible splendor as seen from the rim, and at river level.

It is not just an icon of beauty, however. It is a solemn witness to the mighty power of God, who is not only the omnipotent Creator of all things, but also the avenging Defender of His own holiness.

For the beautiful rock strata of the Canyon, with their evidences of deposition under widespread waters, speak of His world-convulsing judgment at the time of the great Flood. Similarly, the mile-deep Canyon itself, which could never have been carved out by the waters of the present river, tells of a time when a great dammed-up lake full of water from the Flood suddenly broke and a mighty hydraulic monster roared down toward the sea, digging deeply into the path it had chosen along the way.

There it stands today, reminding us of a time in the long ago when *"…the wickedness of man was great in the earth,"* and God said: *"Behold, I am about to destroy them with the earth…I, even I am bringing the flood of water upon the earth…"* (Genesis 6:5,13,17).

Therefore, as people gaze in silent wonder at its unique magnificence, they should remember the words of the psalmist, *"Be still, and know that I am God: I will be exalted among the heathen, I will be exalted in the earth."* (Ps. 46:10).

HENRY MORRIS,
CO-AUTHOR OF *THE GENESIS FLOOD*

4

The solemn witness of Grand Canyon (David Toney)

As the great post-Flood continents and mountains began to rise from the waters of a global deluge (Gen. 8:3-5), a huge chasm was formed that is now the Grand Canyon of Arizona. Inland waters, rushing down to newly deepened ocean basins, rapidly excavated the 5,000-foot deep layers of mud, silt, and sand that had been deposited during the year of the Flood. As God describes this in Psalm 104:8, *"The mountains rose, the valleys* [ocean basins] *sank down to the place which You established for them."* And thus, *"At Your rebuke they* [the waters] *fled…they hurried away"* (v. 7).

By this means, God brought into full view the billions of plants and animals that had been preserved through rapid burial during the Flood. These creatures did not die before Adam and Eve sinned, for *"…through one man sin entered into the world, and death through sin… for the creation was subjected to futility, not willingly, but because of Him who subjected it…"* (Rom. 5:12; 8:20).

The Grand Canyon, like every other major geographic feature of this planet, provides an eloquent, though silent, witness to the amazing fact that *"…the world at that time was destroyed,*

(Above) Point Hansbrough, from the Eminence Break Trail in Marble Canyon

(Left) Tapeats Rapid (David Toney)

being flooded with water." (2 Pet. 3:6). May these spectacular visual aids bring us to the feet of our Lord Jesus Christ, who made the world (John 1:3 *"All things came into being through Him, and apart from Him nothing came into being that has come into being."*) and died in our place that we might live with Him forever – John 3:16, *"For God so loved the world, that He gave His only begotten Son, that whoever believes in Him shall not perish, but have eternal life."*

JOHN WHITCOMB,
CO-AUTHOR OF *THE GENESIS FLOOD*

The Grand Canyon is an awesome display of God's creation. Carved through limestone, sandstone, shale, schist, and granite, this great chasm stretches 277 miles through the Colorado Plateau. It descends over a mile into the earth and extends as much as 18 miles in width. The Canyon holds within its walls mountains that are taller than anything east of the Mississippi River. Grand Canyon National Park encompasses both Marble Canyon and Grand Canyon.

The Grand Canyon is also a place to find and explore the wonders of His creation. When viewed from a biblical perspective, the Canyon has "God" written all over it, from the splendor and grandeur of the Canyon walls, to the intelligent design of the Creator displayed in the creatures that inhabit this magical place.

Not only is the Canyon a testimony to creation, but it also presents evidence of God's judgment of the world, as told in the book of Genesis. It was a judgment by water of a world broken by the sin of man known as "the Fall." (See the Genesis account of the Days of Creation, the Fall, and the Flood on pages 10-11.) The Canyon gives us a glimpse of the effects of a catastrophic global flood, as well as an appreciation for the scale of the biblical Flood of Noah's day. And yet, at the same time, we see God's handiwork in the beauty and majesty of the earth that we live in today.

Visitors to the Grand Canyon generally find it to be awe inspiring, but at the same time, too overwhelming to be fully understood on its own, for the Canyon can't tell us about itself. As humans, we tend to ask two questions as we view this vast, mysterious

(Left) The tranquil falls of Elves Chasm

(Bottom Left) Desert bighorn sheep, common visitors to the Canyon's depths

(Below) Chuckwallas can reach 16 inches in length.

6

hole in the ground: how and why. With the help of some of the top creation scientists and theologians from around the world, we hope to at least scratch the surface of these questions and provide you with some resources to "dig deeper" if you wish.

If we visit the Canyon, or read the prevailing interpretive literature about it, we will find that the views presented are predominantly based on evolutionary theories. For the Canyon, this means that the rock layers were laid down a particle at a time over literally hundreds of millions of years and that the Canyon was later carved slowly by the Colorado River. These theories tend to deny God's involvement and often His very existence.

As you read this book, you will see that we look at the Canyon from a biblical worldview. With that in mind, there is one basic premise, or framework, used as a starting point. That premise is: the Bible, in its original form, is the inerrant Word of God. Therefore, there are three truths that should be clarified. First, in Genesis a "day" is a day, which means a literal 24-hour period of time (technically a "solar day" which is approximately 24 hours). Genesis 1:5 says *"… And there was evening and there was morning, one day."* Second, there was no death before sin. The first death came as a result of initial sin

Marble Canyon

in Genesis 3:21: *"The Lord God made garments of skin for Adam and his wife, and clothed them."* And third, Noah's flood was an actual historical global event. Genesis 7:19-20 says, *"The water prevailed more and more upon the earth, so that all the high mountains everywhere under the heavens were covered. The water prevailed fifteen cubits [about 20 feet] higher, and the mountains were covered."*

If we accept those truths, then Scripture tells us that God created the heavens and earth, and everything in them in six literal days. Based on the lineages laid out in the Bible and other historical documents, this occurred about 6,000 years ago. The vast majority of the sedimentary layers we see in the Grand Canyon, and in the rest of the world for that matter, were deposited as the result of a global flood that occurred after, and ultimately as a result of, the initial sin that took place in the Garden of Eden. And the fossils found in the rock layers are remnants of the plants and animals that perished in the Flood.

Other interpretations — that there was a "gap" early in Genesis 1, that creation days were "long periods of time," or that it was just a

"local flood" — are compromise positions, compromises made in an attempt to fit man's fallible ideas into what God has told us in His Word. Deuteronomy 4:2 says, *"You shall not add to the Word which I am commanding you…"*

Unfortunately, these compromises do just that. They add to God's Word in an effort to fit man's millions-of-years evolutionary theories into the Bible. This compromise in turn calls into question the authority of Scripture, beginning in the first verse of Genesis right through the last verse of Revelation.

Some will say that the age of the earth is not important, that it is a "non-essential," but what is vital is a belief in and a personal relationship with the living God. To some degree that is true. The gates to heaven will not be closed to

(Above) Fluting in the Vishnu Schist along river's edge

(Left) Grand Canyon rattlesnake

(Bottom Left) Sacred datura

us for believing in millions of years. But it is important! Why? Because adding millions of years to the Bible undermines the authority of the Word of God. If we can't believe the accounts of Genesis, which are foundational to the entire Bible, why would

8

we believe the rest to be truth? If the Word doesn't really mean "in six days," then maybe it doesn't really mean "thou shall not… "

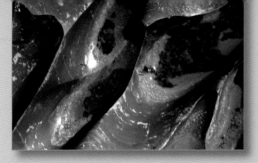

(Above) Polished Redwall Limestone

Realize also that the age of the earth is the cornerstone of evolution. Without an earth that is millions of years old, the entire molecules-to-man theory of evolution falls apart. Without millions of years of supposed mutations and adaptations, reptiles can't grow feathers and "learn" to fly. Without millions of years, the human eye, with all its complexities, does not have time to evolve. Without millions of years, man is then forced to consider a Creator, a Creator to whom he just may be accountable.

The evolutionist will read this and say, "That is *just* a religious point of view." Not true. It is a world view. Religion, as defined in the dictionary, is "any system of belief, practices, ethical values, etc…. (humanism is a religion)." By that definition, both humanism and evolution are as much a religion as Christianity. They are all systems of belief. The issue at hand is not what "religion" we believe in, but rather how it affects our view of the world in which we live.

Both groups, the evolutionists and the creationists, look at the same data, only from a different perspective or world view. The creationist assumes a young earth as God's Word indicates, versus the evolutionist who assumes an earth millions of years old based on man's theories. When we break down the two theories of how the Grand Canyon was formed, it seems that the biggest difference is the amount of time and water. The evolutionists' view is that a little bit of water eroded the Canyon over a long period of time through hard rock. The creationists' view is that a whole lot of water over a relatively short amount of time cut the Canyon through layers laid down by the Flood. But the bigger difference is in how the layers were formed in the first place. Was it millions of years of slow, particle-at-a-time deposition, or catastrophic deposition during a global flood?

What it really comes down to is whether we put our faith in the book given to us by God, or in the books written by man.

May you find this look at the Grand Canyon, from *A Different View*, to be a blessing and a window into His world.

(Right) Four-inch fishhook cactus crowned in blooms

(Below) Day's light in Marble Canyon

In the beginning God created the heavens and the earth. The earth was formless and void, and darkness was over the surface of the deep, and the Spirit of God was moving over the surface of the waters.

Then God said, "Let there be light"; and there was light…God called the light day, and the darkness He called night. And there was evening and there was morning, one day.

Then God said, "Let there be an expanse in the midst of the waters, and let it separate the waters from the waters." …God called the expanse heaven. And there was evening and there was morning, a second day.

Then God said, "Let the waters below the heavens be gathered into one place, and let the dry land appear"; and it was so. God called the dry land earth, and the gathering together of the waters He called seas; and God saw that it was good.

Then God said, "Let the earth sprout vegetation: plants yielding seed, and fruit trees on the earth bearing fruit after their kind with seed in them"; and it was so…And God saw that it was good. There was evening and there was morning, a third day.

…Then God said, "Let there be lights in the expanse of the heavens…" …God made the two great lights, the greater light to govern the day, and the lesser light to govern the night; He made the stars also…And God saw that it was good. There was evening and there was morning, a fourth day.

Then God said, "Let the waters teem with swarms of living creatures, and let birds fly above the earth…" And God saw that it was good…There was evening and there was morning, a fifth day.

Then God said, "Let the earth bring forth living creatures after their kind: cattle and creeping things and beasts of the earth after their kind"; and it was so… Then God said, "Let Us make man in Our image, according to Our likeness…" In the image of God He created him; male and female He created them…God saw all that He had made, and behold, it was very good. And there was evening and there was morning, the sixth day.

Thus the heavens and the earth were completed, and all their hosts…and He rested on the seventh day from all His work which He had done

(Gen. 1:1-2:3).

THE FALL

Then the Lord God took the man and put him into the garden of Eden to cultivate it and keep it. The Lord God commanded the man, saying, "From any tree of the garden you may eat freely; but from the tree of the knowledge of good and evil you shall not eat, for in the day that you eat from it you will surely die."...When the woman saw that the tree was good for food, and that it was a delight to the eyes, and that the tree was desirable to make one wise, she took from its fruit and ate; and she gave also to her husband with her, and he ate. Then the eyes of both of them were opened...The Lord God said..."Because you have...eaten from the tree about which I commanded you, saying, 'You shall not eat from it'; cursed is the ground because of you; in toil you will eat of it all the days of your life. Both thorns and thistles it shall grow for you; and you will eat the plants of the field; by the sweat of your face you will eat bread, till you return to the ground, because from it you were taken; for you are dust, and to dust you shall return." (Genesis 2:15-3:19)

THE FLOOD

[About 1,500 years later.]

Then the Lord saw that the wickedness of man was great on the earth...The Lord was sorry that He had made man on the earth...The Lord said, "I will blot out man whom I have created from the face of the land, from man to animals to creeping things and to birds of the sky; for I am sorry that I have made them." But Noah found favor in the eyes of the Lord.

...Then God said to Noah..."Make for yourself an ark...the length of the ark [shall be] three hundred cubits [450 feet], its breadth fifty cubits [75 feet], and its height thirty cubits [45 feet]...Behold, I, even I am bringing the flood of water upon the earth, to destroy all flesh in which is the breath of life, from under heaven; everything that is on the earth shall perish. But I will establish My covenant with you; and you shall enter the ark—you and your sons and your wife, and your sons' wives with you. And of every living thing of all flesh, you shall bring two of every kind into the ark, to keep them alive with you; they shall be male and female."... Thus Noah did; according to all that God had commanded him.

...It came about after the seven days, that the water of the flood came upon the earth...All the fountains of the great deep burst open, and the floodgates of the sky were opened. The rain fell upon the earth for forty days and forty nights...The water prevailed more and more upon the earth, so that all the high mountains everywhere under the heavens were covered.

...But God remembered Noah and all the beasts and all the cattle that were with him in the ark; and God caused a wind to pass over the earth, and the water subsided...Also the fountains of the deep and the floodgates of the sky were closed... In the seventh month, on the seventeenth day of the month, the ark rested upon the mountains of Ararat.

...Then God spoke to Noah, saying, "Go out of the ark, you and your wife and your sons and your sons' wives with you. Bring out with you every living thing of all flesh that is with you... that they may...be fruitful and multiply on the earth."

...Then Noah built an altar to the Lord...and the Lord said to Himself, "I will never again curse the ground on account of man, for the intent of man's heart is evil from his youth..."

...Then God spoke to Noah and to his sons with him, saying... "I establish My covenant with you; and all flesh shall never again be cut off by the water of the flood, neither shall there again be a flood to destroy the earth." God said..."When the bow [rainbow] is in the cloud, then I will look upon it, to remember the everlasting covenant between God and every living creature of all flesh that is on the earth." (Genesis 6:5-9:17)

I set My bow in the cloud, and it shall be for a sign of a covenant between Me and the earth. It shall come about, when I bring a cloud over the earth, that the bow will be seen in the cloud, and I will remember My covenant, which is between Me and you and every living creature of all flesh; and never again shall the water become a flood to destroy all flesh. – Genesis 9:13-15

Many in the secular and Christian worlds have claimed that the Flood described in the Bible in Genesis 6-9 was just a local event (or even myth). Not only does the language of the Bible describe a global cataclysmic event (the highest hills under the whole of heaven were covered by water), but the covenant of the rainbow dictates that this event of Noah's day was not just some local inundation.

Since the time of Noah, there have been *thousands* of local floods. In fact, numerous such local events occur every year in most countries. However, the God of the Bible made a covenant between Himself and the Earth. He promised that whenever a rainbow appeared, it would be a reminder that He would never again bring such a flood (a global flood) on the Earth. If Noah's flood was just a local event, then it means that God breaks His promise every time a flood occurs somewhere on the earth.

Although we don't have to be concerned about another global flood, we do have to be ready for another global catastrophe, which will be by fire. In 2 Peter 3, Peter warns that just as God judged with a flood, one day there will be a final judgment by fire. One day, God will again destroy the Earth, but He will remake it to be perfect once again. Those who have put their faith and trust in the Lord Jesus Christ will live forever with the God of creation in the new heavens and earth.

KEN HAM

I set My bow in the cloud . . .
– Genesis 9:13

12

God's promise over the Canyon

(Above) Calm, reflective waters of the Little Colorado River (Bill Hoesch)

(Right) Turquoise water at the confluence of the Little Colorado River

Surely My hand founded the earth, and My right hand spread out the heavens; when I call to them, they stand together. – Isaiah 48:13

Behold, He comes with the clouds, and
every eye will see Him . . . – Revelation 1:7

14

(Left) Winter clouds from Maricopa Point, South Rim (David Toney)

Fern Glen Arch (Joe Pollock)

T he Bible says that the evidence of God's existence is seen in the things that He has made, and I confirm that in my studies as a scientist.

ANDREW SNELLING

For since the creation of the world His invisible attributes, His eternal power and divine nature, have been clearly seen, being understood through what has been made, so that they are without excuse. – Romans 1:20

(Right) The growth of these six-inch "dog-tooth" calcium carbonate crystals in a geode-like solution cavity in the Redwall Limestone displays God's creative genius. (Jacque Kewalramani)

And God called the light day, and the darkness He called night. And the evening and the morning were the first day.

– Genesis 1:5

The dating of rocks by the radioactive decay of certain minerals is undoubtedly the main argument today for the dogma of an old earth.

But the Bible clearly teaches a recent creation of both the heavens and the earth, so Christians have often tried to reinterpret this doctrine to accommodate the long ages required by radioactive dating. For those Christians who believe that Genesis (like the other historical books of the Bible) should be understood as literal history, it has therefore been necessary to show the fallacies in the so-called "scientific proofs" of an old earth.

HENRY MORRIS

17

On the glorious splendor of your majesty and on your wonderful works, I will meditate. – Psalm 145:5

Morning fog in Marble Canyon

In fact, the Grand Canyon is one of the most striking natural objects in the world. Everybody can find here something interesting and important for himself. Whereas laymen admire the wonderful views, specialists in natural sciences are attracted by the unique geological setting. It is possible to see a continuous sequence of sedimentary strata lying on top of the oldest rock in the Canyon, referred to as the "basement" rock, capped by the youngest rocks in the Canyon, the lava flows of the Uinkaret Plateau. Thus, a geologist descending from the Canyon rim to the river's edge can research, step by step, an entire sequence of events.

ALEX LALOMOV

Descent along the Kaibab Trail (Keith Swenson)

John Wesley Powell wrote about Redwall Cavern on his exploration in 1869: "The water sweeps rapidly in this elbow of river, and has cut its way under the rock, excavating a vast half-circular chamber, which, if utilized for a theater, would give sitting to 50,000 people." A slight exaggeration of its actual size, it could realistically only seat 5,000.

Thus says God the Lord, Who created the heavens and stretched them out, Who spread out the earth and its offspring, Who gives breath to the people on it and spirit to those who walk in it, "I am the Lord . . ." – Isaiah 42:5, 6

(Above) Redwall Cavern from upstream (Joe Pollock)

(Right) People in cavern (Courtesy of Arizona River Runners)

(Below) The inner depths of Redwall Cavern (Tom Vail)

Be still and know that I am God . . .

– Psalm 46:10

After many years of intense study of the problem of origins from a scientific viewpoint, I am convinced that the facts of science declare special creation to be the only rational explanation of origins.

"In the beginning God created . . ." is still the most up-to-date statement that can be made about origins.

DUANE GISH

21

Early in the history of geology, it was common to appeal to the Flood described in the Bible to explain the origin of most or all rocks and fossils. Noah's flood was typically recognized as a catastrophic global event. The earth's crust was pictured by some as dynamic and capable of rapid vertical and horizontal motions on

Cross-bedding is also seen in the Supai Formation. (Chuck Hill)

local, regional, and global scales. However, Noah's flood began to play an increasingly less important role in historical geology during the nineteenth century. Theories of gradualism increased in popularity as theories of catastrophism waned. Ideas of past catastrophic geology were replaced with ideas of uniformitarianism, which relies on constancy of present gradual physical processes and that "the present is the key to the past." Ideas of global-scale dynamics were replaced with ideas of local erosion, deposition, extrusion, and intrusion.

Fossilized brachiopod (Joe Pollock)

However, towards the end of the twentieth century, many geologists began to realize that present gradual physical processes could not produce the features observed in many rock layers. They thus began to again invoke catastrophic processes, such as storms, floods, explosive eruptions and meteorite or asteroid impacts. Indeed, the mass destruction of myriads of animals and plants and their burial around the globe at the same relative levels in the geologic record unmistakably testifies to global-scale catastrophic processes. The nautiloids found in the Redwall Limestone through portions of the Grand Canyon are evidence of a mass destruction and burial. Also, many strata are now known to cover vast areas across the continents, with distinctive features such as cross-bedding that are recognized indicators of rapid sediment transport on a massive scale by swift currents in deep water. This is easily seen in the sandstones in the Grand Canyon.

Furthermore, fossilized seashells exposed high in mountain ranges that are still rising today (such as the Himalayas) testify to sediment layers deposited on the sea floor having been uplifted many miles vertically. This is also true of the Kaibab Limestone, the uppermost layer of the Grand Canyon. Thick sequences of sediment layers, as seen in the Tapeats Sandstone, the lowest of the flood deposited layers, are found that have been folded while still soft very soon after deposition, indicative of all the deposition and the

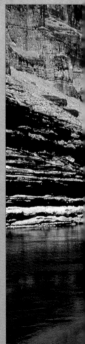

upheaval responsible for the folding being one event. And finally, most rock layers in many sequences show no evidence of erosion between the deposition of each layer, signifying continuous deposition of those whole sequences, whereas much of today's land surface was seemingly eroded rapidly by vast sheets of swiftly moving water draining off the continents.

Collectively, all this evidence is overwhelmingly consistent with much of the geologic record, at least the portion that contains most all the visible fossils, having been catastrophically deposited, extruded, uplifted and eroded during the globally dynamic biblical Flood.

ANDREW SNELLING

Fold in the Tapeats Sandstone

Layers seen in Conquistador Aisle
(Chuck Hill)

24

When biblical creationists/flood geologists offer explanations for the rock layers in the Grand Canyon, they appeal neither to biblical authority (the Bible doesn't mention the Grand Canyon!) nor to mystical or supernatural processes. They appeal, instead, directly to the evidence we can see, touch, and measure. That evidence seems to suggest that processes we do understand, like turbidity currents, explain what we see — except that the evidence also tells us that the scale was regional, continental, or even global, not just local.

GARY PARKER

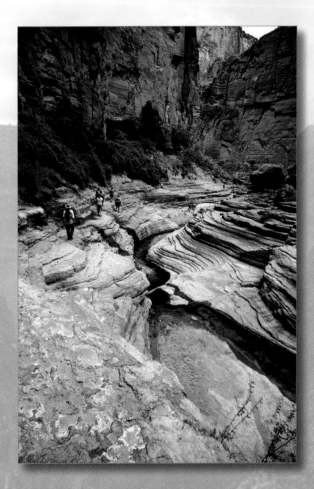

(Left) Afternoon light settles in the Granite Gorge of Grand Canyon

(Right) The alluring Matkatamiba Canyon (Joe Pollock)

This photo brings back memories of a very pleasant evening in the Grand Canyon. One spring in the late 1980s, I was leading a backpacking group going down Hance Creek Trail to the Colorado. The trail is beautiful but rugged, and we took several side trips to points of geologic interest. By the time we reached Hance Rapid on the evening of the third day, we were no longer especially enthused about eating more freeze-dried food out of our backpacks.

For that reason we were looking forward to an evening rendezvous with a river rafting group. Not only would there be great Christian fellowship as the two groups became acquainted, but the raft crew would serve us real food! The rafting groups have a well-deserved reputation for good meals, and almost any fresh and hot food tastes terrific to weary backpackers.

The food and fellowship surpassed our expectations. The evening weather was perfect, neither too hot nor too cold. Many people, including myself, decided not to pitch tents, but instead, laid our sleeping bags on the soft sand and prepared to sleep under the stars.

Several of the people around me shared an interest in astronomy, so we swapped star lore as the sun set. Soon we could see that our beach faced almost north, because the North Star appeared just above the wall of the Inner Gorge, directly across the river from us. The Big Dipper was upside down, with its guide stars pointing to the North Star, and its handle was stretched out almost horizontally to our right, to the east. I knew that as the night wore on, the Dipper and other stars would rotate around the North Star counterclockwise as the earth turned eastward, which is what made the star-circles in this time-lapse photo.

So the handle of the Big Dipper was like a big clock God had provided for us, marking off each hour with a fifteen-degree rotation toward the west. The night sky became very dark and clear, bringing out all the various glories of the stars. As I gazed up into deep heaven, I was contemplating how God might have brought the light from distant stars

He counts the number of the stars; He gives names to all of them.
— Psalms 147:4

(Upper) Time-lapsed tracking of stars around the North Star (David Toney) and (lower) from a different angle (Jacque Kewalramani)

(Right) Sunset over the Canyon

and galaxies to the Earth within a day, in time for Adam and Eve to see the Milky Way and the galaxy in Andromeda on that glorious evening on the sixth day of creation. The soft roar of the rapid lulled me to sleep. Each time I awoke through the night, God's great clock in the heavens was always there to tell me the time.

After that experience, I continued thinking about how God brought the light from distant galaxies to the earth very quickly and developed a model of how that could have happened. As a result, I presented the outline of a creationist cosmology at the Third International Conference on Creationism and later wrote a book, *Starlight and Time*, on the subject. My experiences in the Grand Canyon stimulated my encounters with God's creation and contributed greatly to that work.

RUSS HUMPHREYS

27

They who dwell in the ends of the earth stand in awe of Your signs; You make the dawn and the sunset shout for joy. – Psalm 65:8

The Grand Canyon's breathtaking beauty tends to make us ignore the sky above it. It's just a backdrop, a scenic contrast enabling the shimmering waters below to more elegantly reflect the Canyon's grandeur. But soar way above the Canyon in your mind's eye, through the sky and beyond. The atmosphere's mix of gases enables the biosphere to live and breathe. The ozone layer protects life against damaging ultraviolet radiation. The Earth's magnetic field protects us against harmful cosmic radiation. The planet's amazingly precise position in space, hung "upon nothing" (Job 26:7, *"He stretches out the north over empty space and hangs the earth on nothing"*), ensures that we neither boil nor freeze by being too close or too far away from the sun. The Earth's angle of tilt gives us the seasons. After the great Flood, to which the Canyon gives such eloquent testimony, God promised mankind that these seasons "shall not cease" while this present Earth remains.

CARL WIELAND

While the earth remains, seedtime and harvest, and cold and heat, and summer and winter, and day and night shall not cease. – Genesis 8:22

Reflection of grandeur in Marble Canyon

*Ah Lord God! Behold, Thou hast made
the heavens and the earth by Thy great
power and by Thine outstretched arm!
Nothing is too difficult for Thee . .*

. – Jeremiah 32:17

*L*et this be a sign among you, so that when your children
ask later, saying, 'What do these stones mean to you?' then
you shall say to them . . . — Joshua 4:6-7

In the book of Joshua, from the Old Testament, the Lord
commanded Joshua to build a memorial of 12 stones to remind
fathers to teach their children what the Lord had done. In
Joshua, the stones reminded the Israelites that God held the
waters of the Jordan River back, allowing them to cross over
on dry land, after His deliverance of the Israelites from Egypt.

The "stones" of the Grand Canyon are also a memorial, a
memorial placed there by God to remind fathers to teach their
children what He has done – that as a result of sin, He judged the
earth with a global Flood.

To the evolutionist, the river is the primal force in the formation
of the Grand Canyon. Some theorize that over the last 70 million
years, the river has carved through solid rock to form the Canyon
we see today. They believe that this slow carving has been in concert
with the uplifting of the Colorado Plateau allowing the Canyon to
be formed through, and not around, the Kaibab Upwarp, a broad
uplifted feature of the Colorado Plateau. Prior to Glen Canyon Dam,
the river transported as much as 500,000 tons of sediment
per day, which is about five tons per second. When we do
the math based on the erosion rates and sediment load of
the Colorado River, we find a major problem.

Where did all that material go? During those
70 million years the river should have eroded a layer

(Above) Fluting in the basement
rocks of Grand Canyon

(Right) Water-eroded hollows
(Joe Pollock)

30

more than five miles thick off the top of the entire 137,800 square-mile drainage area of the Colorado River. This massive amount of material is nowhere to be found between the Canyon and the sea, as we would expect.

A more popular theory since the late 1950s is that of "stream capturing." This theory speculates that the water of the Colorado River drained out through the Little Colorado River drainage to the east or through the Kanab Creek drainage to the north. Then only about six million years ago, a "gully" was eroded back through the Colorado Plateau from the west by a process called headward erosion. This new gully, or canyon, then "captured" the Colorado, changing its course to flow through what is now known as the Grand Canyon. According to the stream capturing theory, the plateau has since been uplifted so that both drainages now drain into the Colorado River.

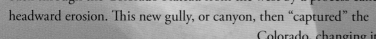

The river scours the rocks as it searches for a path to the sea.

Zoroaster Granite intrusions (pink) in the Vishnu Schist (black) in Granite Gorge

A different view is that the layers through which the Grand Canyon is carved show classic flood-plain geology on a very, very large scale. Nine major sedimentary layers are seen throughout the Canyon and, in fact, some of them are found to cover much of the North American continent. What is unique about the Grand Canyon is that these layers are exposed for all to see, exposed all the way down to the basement rocks of schist and granite. These basement rocks, although probably not in their original form, are thought to be part of the original creation. Also exposed are some of the pre-Flood deposits that were likely laid down when God separated the land from the sea. ("*…Let the waters below the heavens be gathered into one place, and let the dry land appear…*" Genesis 1:9.)

The creationists' view of the carving of the Canyon is that it took place after, or possibly during, the receding of the Flood. As the floodwaters drew back, they likely took with them much of the sediment that was initially laid down. Although there wasn't anyone there to witness the event, one theory is that as the waters receded, some very large land-locked lakes were left just north and east of the Canyon area behind natural dams formed by the Kaibab Upwarp. These lakes eventually breached those dams, causing a flood that carved the Canyon in a series of catastrophic events, a carving that took but a few days, not millions of years. Some reject the breached dam theory, suggesting instead that the carving was done as part of the receding of the Flood itself.

The one thing both creationists and evolutionists do agree on is that it was water that eroded the Grand Canyon. Again, since no one was there to witness these events, it is difficult to say exactly how the

Canyon was formed. But in the creationists' view, the carving of the Canyon would have taken place catastrophically, with the erosion process quickly and easily cutting through the layers laid down by the flood.

One thing that is fairly obvious is that when the sedimentary layers were still soft, there was a significant amount of shifting in

Folding of the Tapeats Sandstone in Carbon Creek (Note the people in the foreground of the upper picture.)

the underlying basement rock. This is observed, for example, along the fault in Carbon Canyon, a dry creek tributary to the Grand Canyon. Here, as seen in the picture at left, the layers are "folded" without breaking. As we see during earthquakes today, when hard rock is moved along a fault, it cracks — it doesn't bend!

In the areas that have not been shifted vertically, the sedimentary layers still lie relatively horizontal and show essentially no sign of any physical erosion or chemical weathering between the layers. The evolutionary model says that each layer was exposed for millions of years before the layer above was deposited. If that were true, why don't we see evidence of erosion? What we do see between most of the layers is a very clear, distinct, straight line that is unwavering for miles.

The Canyon is often considered the "holy land" to the geologist. And rightfully so, as it is a grand cathedral, carved in the rocks by water that has eroded, fluted, and polished the walls into shapes fitting for a cathedral. Nowhere else on earth is so much geology exposed and accessible to study. And nowhere else is there such compelling evidence of a young earth that was inundated by a global Flood.

If you examine the geology of the Grand Canyon with an open mind, I believe you will see how the evidence points to a young earth. May you find it enlightening and thought-provoking.

33

(Above) A still pool reflects the layers in North Canyon.

(Right) Cooling pattern in a lava flow in the western Canyon

(Lower left) Small rocks swirled by the river's current erode "potholes" along the water's edge.

Not too many decades before John Wesley Powell explored the Grand Canyon for the first time in 1869, the dominant view in the Christian world of Europe and America was that God created the world in six 24-hour days about 4,000 BC. About 1,600 years later, according to this view, the earth was judged with a global catastrophic flood at the time of Noah. In the late 18th century, different histories of the Earth began to be developed and popularized, most of which were naturalistic in character. These theories sought to explain the origin and history of the earth by appealing only to time, chance, and the laws of nature working on matter. God was denied, or at least His Word was left out of the picture, in constructing a history of the Earth.

The Scotsman James Hutton (1726-97) was a doctor and farmer before eventually becoming interested in geology. In his *Theory of the Earth* (1795), he proposed that the continents were gradually being eroded into the ocean basins. These sediments were then very slowly hardened and raised by the internal heat of the earth to form new continents, which would be gradually eroded into the ocean again. This cyclical process had gone on maybe forever, according to Hutton.

The English drainage engineer William Smith (1769-1839) became known as the "Father of English Stratigraphy" because he produced the first geological maps of England and Wales and developed the method of using fossils to assign relative dates to the strata. As a "catastrophist," he too imagined that the Earth was much older than the Bible taught.

Charles Lyell (1797-1875), a lawyer-turned-geologist, began to dominate geological thinking with his three-volume *Principles of Geology* (1830-33). Building on Hutton's ideas, Lyell insisted that the geological features of the earth can, and indeed must, be explained by gradual processes of erosion, sedimentation, and deformation operating over millions of years at essentially the same rate and power as we observe today. He rejected any notion of regional or global catastrophism, and his uniformitarian assumptions became the ruling dogma in geology.

These uniformitarian and catastrophist views of earth history were opposed by a number of writers who became known as the "scriptural geologists." These scientists and non-scientists raised biblical, philosophical, and geological objections to these old-earth theories and defended Genesis 1-11 as the true history of the early period of the creation. But their arguments were ignored by their old-earth proponents.

The scriptural geologists were not opposed to geological facts, but to the old-earth interpretations of those facts, which they argued were based on anti-biblical philosophical

assumptions. In this they were correct. Hutton was a deist or secret atheist. Smith and Lyell were probably deists or some sort of vague theists. These old-earth theorists were not objective, unbiased, let-the-facts-speak-for-themselves observers of the physical evidence. They all rejected the history revealed in Scripture and operated with the assumptions of philosophical naturalism in their interpretation of the geological evidence.

So the Genesis-geology debate was, and still is, a conflict of worldviews. The Scriptural geologists of today find that the evidence in the Grand Canyon confirms the Word of God. Many use the Canyon as "Exhibit A" in their defense of the authority of Scripture against vague forms of theism, atheism, and deism that continue to deny a biblical worldview.

TERRY
MORTENSON

Sunset over "Exhibit A"

Before we can properly understand geology, we need to know the earth's history. Unlike secular geologists, creationist geologists don't need to speculate about history because we accept the eyewitness accounts of past events, preserved in a reliable written record – the Bible.

Although the Bible is not a "geology" book, it allows us to understand the big geological picture when we are alert for geological clues. For each historical event we simply ask, "How would this have affected the geology of the earth? What would we look for today?"

From such a study, we conclude that most rocks we see on Earth today would have been formed during two very short periods of time. The first was the six-day creation week, about 6,000 years ago when the entire planet was produced. The second was the one-year Flood when the planet was reshaped. By comparison, not much happened geologically in the roughly 1,500-year period between creation and the Flood, or in the roughly 4,500-year period since.

A simplified geological model is illustrated in the figure below. The biblical time-line on the left has the most recent time at the top and the earliest at the bottom. The time-scale is divided into four parts: the Creation Event, the Flood Event, the Pre-Flood Era and the Post-Flood Era.

To illustrate how geological process rates varied in the past, we can place another scale alongside the time-scale. This is a rock-scale (center), with the most recently formed rocks at the top, and the earliest at the bottom — the way they occur in the earth. The lengths of the different parts of the rock-scale represent the quantity of rock material found on the earth today in contrast with the lengths of the corresponding parts of the time-scale. The major rock layers found in

GEOLOGIC TIME AND ROCK SCALE

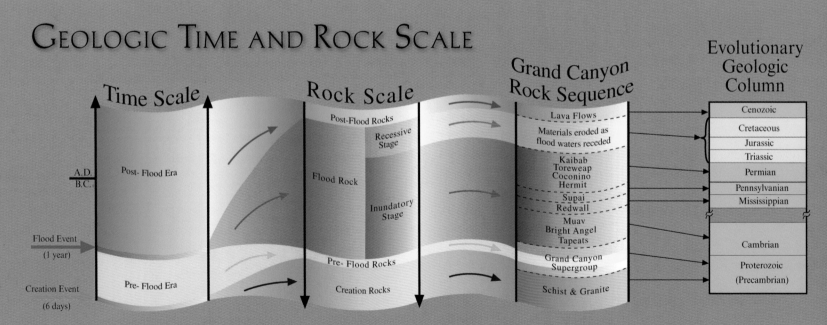

Note: The placement of the beginning and the end of the Flood at an exact level within Grand Canyon is debatable. Most creation scientists place the Flood's commencement either within, or at the base of the Grand Canyon Supergroup. The simplified evolutionary geologic column is shown for reference and is not necessarily to scale.

the Grand Canyon are shown on the right, indicating when they were formed.

To the far right is a simplified evolutionary geologic column for the Grand Canyon. The arrows show where the layers of the Grand Canyon are generally assigned in that model.

For the model to have practical application, the broad framework must be expanded with specific details of the events and processes and their time relationships. This is not difficult. The Flood event, for example, can be divided into two stages: an Inundatory stage with the Floodwaters rising onto the land, and a Recessive stage with the Floodwaters flowing off the land.

Within this geological framework we can interpret the rocks in the field. Every rock on earth today must fit somewhere because the rock-scale covers the entire history of the earth.

View of Palisades of the Desert from Hilltop Ruin (Joe Pollock)

In the walls of the Grand Canyon, horizontal layers of thick strata are exposed. They extend for thousands of square miles across several states of the United States. Because the sedimentary deposits are so huge, it is most unlikely that they were deposited in either the pre- or post-Flood eras. There was not enough time for slow geological processes to deposit such large quantities of sediment. Hence, they must have been deposited in either the creation or Flood event.

However, the horizontal layers comprising the walls of the Canyon contain fossilized remains of corals, shells, sea lilies, snails, and plants. Clearly these were not deposited during creation week; therefore, they must have been destroyed during the Flood.

Animal trackways provide another important clue. Tracks are found in the Supai Group and the Coconino Sandstone. Tracks mean the animals were alive, so the strata must have been deposited before all air-breathing creatures perished. That was before the world was completely covered with water, during the inundatory stage.

So, with this simple model and a little reasoning, we have determined that the horizontal layers were deposited in the first part of the Flood while the waters were advancing. We can use the same approach with the other parts of the Canyon, such as the metamorphosed rocks at the bottom (Creation, pre-Flood or early Flood), the erosion surfaces at the top (Flood recessive), the lava flows (post-Flood), and the carving of the Canyon itself (Flood recessive or post-Flood). Biblical geology is the key to understanding the rocks.

TASMAN WALKER

37

Does radioactive dating prove the rocks in Grand Canyon are millions of years old? Geologists use various dating methods to determine the ages of rocks. While the radioactive (radioisotopic) dating methods include carbon-14, carbon-14 dating cannot be used on rocks generally because it relies on the presence of carbon in organic materials such as charcoal, and is limited to less than 70,000 years. On the other hand, the radioactive dating methods used on rocks and minerals involve radioisotopes with much slower decay rates, and so they usually provide ages of millions and even billions of years.

For example, the Cardenas Basalt lavas found deep within the eastern Grand Canyon are claimed to be 1,070 million years old based on rubidium-strontium dating. Since the lavas cooled, some rubidium atoms in these rocks have been unstable and have radioactively "decayed" into strontium. By careful chemical analyses of the rubidium and strontium atoms involved, and by knowing the present

rate at which this decay occurs, it is supposedly possible to work out how long ago the process started. This, then, should be the time when the lavas cooled, or the "age" of these rocks.

The Cardenas Basalt lavas of the eastern Grand Canyon (Keith Swenson)

However, some crucial assumptions are made. First, that the original quantities of the radioactive elements in the rock, and their decay products, are accurately known. Second, that only radioactive decay has altered the quantities of the radioactive elements and their decay products since the rock formed. In other words, there has been no removal or addition of these elements by ground waters or other weathering and/or alteration processes. And third, that the radioactive decay has been constant at today's measured rates since the rock formed. Even though these assumptions are unproven, and unprovable, they are commonly accepted as correct because they give evolutionary geologists the desired results. Indeed, most people are convinced because these apparently definitive dates are published as fact. But are they? Could the assumptions be wrong?

The Cardenas Basalt lavas have also been dated using the potassium-argon radioactive method, yielding an age of only 516 million years, less than half the 1,070 million years obtained by rubidium-strontium! But seldom do you see the lower number quoted in evolutionary publications as the age of the lavas, because it is generally explained away as an anomaly.

Furthermore, before these basalt lavas erupted, some of the molten rock underground was squeezed between the strata to form diabase sills (thick sheets that parallel the rock layering) which now outcrop in several places along the Colorado River. Interestingly, the diabase sill at Bass Rapids (seen to the right) has been dated using the four main radioactive methods, which should, if the crucial assumptions are correct, all yield close to the same age. The results:

Bass Sill is seen above and is outlined at left.
(Andrew Snelling)

- Potassium-argon . . . . 840 million years
- Rubidium-strontium . . . . 1,055 million years
- Uranium-lead . . . . 1,249 million years
- Samarium-neodymium. . . . . . . 1,375 million years

Conclusion? Because all these radioisotopes have been subject to the same conditions within this diabase sill during and since its formation, it is logically difficult to defend the assumption that the decay rates have been constant in the past. Indeed, the obvious way to explain the gross disagreements between these dates is that the decay rates have been different in the past than they are today. The large inconsistencies among these methods show that they are emphatically not providing reliable absolute dates. Thus, the true age of these Grand Canyon strata may have little connection with the dates that radioactive methods supply. Contrary to what is widely believed, radioactive dating has not proven the rocks of the Grand Canyon to be millions of years old.

ANDREW SNELLING

One of the chief mental barriers to accepting the Grand Canyon's magnificent horizontally bedded layers as the product of a single recent global Flood is the belief that radioisotope (radioactive) dating proves that these layers were deposited hundreds of millions of years ago. This extremely important issue motivated the formation in July 1997 of a research team known as the RATE (Radioisotopes and the Age of The Earth) group. Its primary purpose was to address head-on the conflict between the youthfulness of the

that a straightforward reading of Scripture would indicate, an earth age of millions to billions of years provided by dating methods using long half-life radioisotopes such as uranium and thorium.

The team recognized this as a key issue that must be answered in a credible way if the concept of a recent creation and a global Genesis Flood is to be taken seriously. The RATE research initially focused on the long-age radioisotopes commonly used for dating, but it soon became apparent that carbon-14 (C-14) data, supposedly from very old fossil organisms, also represents an extremely important piece of the puzzle.

Probably the most astounding discovery is that undecayed C-14 appears to be present in material representing fossilized life through the entire geological record! Using the standard C-14 dating assumptions, these analyses seem to require that the origin of life on earth goes no farther back in time than about 70,000 years. When one takes into account the massive changes that a global flood would have caused to the biosphere, the time scale implied by the data collapses to approximately 5,000 years.

This existence of measurable C-14 levels in all sorts of organic samples that should be C-14 "dead" according to the widely accepted geological time scale, is abundantly documented in the standard radiocarbon literature. This is true of essentially all such samples tested since the early 1980s in dozens of highly precise accelerator mass spectrometer (AMS) laboratories around the world. It was also true for the ten carefully selected coal samples, some from the Grand Canyon area, that the RATE team had analyzed using AMS.

Walls of schist and granite in Granite Gorge, which evolutionists date at 1.7 billion years

Foundational to radioisotope dating is the assumption that nuclear decay rates never change. However, the extreme (thousand-fold) conflict between C-14 age determinations and methods based on longer half-life isotopes, such as uranium and potassium, points to the likelihood this assumption is incorrect. Another line of evidence strongly supporting this inference is the large amount of helium (produced by nuclear disintegration of uranium) still retained in tiny zircon crystals in granite rocks. One RATE research project carefully measured the rate that helium migrates through zircon crystals. These measurements indicate that such observed high levels of helium retention in zircon could persist for, *at most*, only a few thousand years. The high helium migration rates measured imply only a few thousand years of earth history could have elapsed since creation.

The basic conclusion of this research is that dating methods utilizing long half-life radioisotopes give an earth age that is incorrect by orders of magnitude. The chief reason is that uniformitarianism — the belief that the present is the key to correctly interpreting the past — *doesn't agree with reality*. In particular, it does not allow for the fact that God intervened in the natural order during creation and during the Flood, as 2 Peter 3:3-6 clearly affirms. The RATE team is convinced this intervention included very high rates of nuclear disintegration relative to what we observe today. We believe there now exists a substantial body of evidence supporting our interpretation of the radioisotope data and are persuaded this evidence points to both a young earth and a recent global Flood.

JOHN BAUMGARDNER

Raven

41

The contact between the dark-colored Hermit Shale and the overlying Coconino sandstone is seen throughout the Canyon. Note the "knife-edge" bedding plane between the totally different rock types in the picture (below), with the white Coconino Sandstone overlying the red Hermit Shale.

The Hermit Shale is thought to have accumulated as silt and mud in a deep ocean environment. It contains index fossils (fossils used by evolutionists to date sedimentary rock) which date it at about 280 million years of age.

The overlying Coconino Sandstone, dated at about 270 million years by evolutionists, tells a different story, although its history is in dispute. Most uniformitarian geologists interpret it as a desert sand-dune deposit, now solidified into hard rock. They base this interpretation on the presence throughout the rock of inclined planes (called cross-bedding) found at an angle to the horizontal bedding of the rock unit as a whole.

Other geologists interpret these very same cross-beds as the product of an underwater sand dune. They base their contention on certain features more representative of wet sand than dry sand, such as the angle of the cross-beds, presence of amphibian tracks fossilized in the sand, features of the sand grains, etc. The underwater case would probably be convincing to all, if it weren't for certain implications which necessarily follow. The average size of the sand grains implies a water velocity of more than three feet per second at the base of a thick column of water at least 100 feet deep. Rapidly moving water on the bottom implies a watery catastrophe on the surface beyond our experience. Based on the angle of cross-bedding and the presence of amphibian tracks, the evidence clearly favors the underwater model. But that water involved an incredible destruction of at least a sizeable part of the continent. Those who advocate the desert interpretation illustrate the maxim, *"I wouldn't have seen it if I hadn't believed it."*

Regardless of how the Coconino was deposited, it originated in a completely different way than the Hermit, and according to evolution, was separated in time by about 10 million years. If the

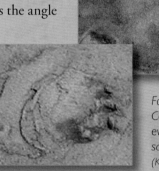

Knife-edge contact between the red Hermit Shale topped by Coconino Sandstone (Keith Swenson)

Fossilized tracks in the Coconino Sandstone give evidence to an underwater sand dune deposit. (Keith Swenson)

Coconino represents a desert (one which covered over 100,000 square miles, by the way), then the ocean bottom which accumulated the Hermit material had to be uplifted, out of water, to an elevation high enough and dry enough to be a desert. Can you imagine the erosion which would take place over this gigantic area, particularly as it was near sea level? And yet, the upper surface of the Hermit is exceptionally flat, with no evidence of normal erosion. It is not possible, as far as has been observed, for these kinds of erosional processes to scour off all possible overlying sediment and leave behind a completely flat Hermit surface on which the Coconino desert could form.

The existence of the sharp, knife-edge contact between those two beds argues against the passage of long periods of time between their depositions. If it weren't for the assumption of evolution, these two beds would speak either of continuous, rapid deposition, or of rapid deposition of the Coconino after an episode of "sheet erosion." In both cases, we're talking about a flood on the scale of the Genesis Flood.

The rocks simply do not support vast ages passing between the deposition of adjacent layers.

JOHN MORRIS

43

The sharp contact between layers, as seen along the Bright Angel Trail, argues against the passage of long periods of time. (Keith Swenson)

One of the most interesting geological features of Grand Canyon strata is the so-called Great Unconformity, the boundary between the lower sedimentary layers and underlying metamorphic and igneous basement rocks. (Note the flat erosional surface in the picture.) Geologists who believe in an old earth contend that the gap between the basement rock and the sedimentation layer, the Great Unconformity, represents more than one billion years of "missing" material. Is that so?

Every homemaker knows that a thin layer of dust forms during just a day or two. After a few years with no cleaning, the layer will be thick enough to grow grass. And eventually, we should see soil with bushes and small trees growing. The Great Unconformity has neither ancient soil nor significant chemical weathering directly beneath it. These stones say to us that the gap was not a long period, at least not millions of years. Do you see the incredible significance of this?

The present-day erosion forms we see include abundant channeling, canyons, and valleys. Maybe then, all evidences of a long gap were deleted by

subsequent erosion. In the Great Unconformity we see nearly planar (flat) erosion of the basement rock surface. This strong rock was smoothed by a tremendous water flow in what appears to be a short period of time. It is likely that this event was what we know as the Genesis Flood.

ALEX LALOMOV

The Great Unconformity supposedly represents more than one billion years of "missing" material. Is that so? (Tom Vail)

The western Grand Canyon contains a unique and spectacular sequence of volcanic flows. The basaltic flows are particularly captivating because of their stark contrasting jet-black color against the light brown and red hues of the underlying sedimentary rocks. These flows appear as "frozen" lava falls cascading down the walls of the inner gorge to the Colorado River below. They also have a much more unique aspect which was first observed by John Wesley Powell in 1869. Powell noted that many of the inner gorge flows are horizontally bedded, indicating that they once extended across the entire width of the inner gorge, damming the Colorado River and forming an immense lake within the Grand Canyon. Later geologic studies showed that there were possibly several separate lava flows within the western Grand Canyon, creating as many as 13 lava dams.

Several important geologic features, which were previously overlooked, give strong indication that the relatively recent lava dams of the western Grand Canyon formed rapidly and were destroyed catastrophically, most likely within several tens to hundreds of years after formation. The entire span of time from the formation of the first dam to the destruction of the last dam could have transpired over a time frame of well under 2,000 years.

The most apparent indication that these dams were short-lived is the absence of lake-deposited sediments within the Grand Canyon. The largest lake would have formed behind a nearly 2,000-foot-high

Lava flows appear as "frozen" falls cascading down the walls of the western Grand Canyon. (Joe Pollock)

lava structure known as Prospect Dam. The water of Prospect Lake would have inundated the inner gorge and covered the flat-lying Tonto Plateau up to the base of the Redwall Limestone below Grand Canyon Village. The lake would have backed up into the myriad of side canyons throughout the Canyon. But where are the remnants of the sediments that would have been deposited into the lake and eventually filled it completely? Lake-deposited sediments should be preserved in thousands of locations. But when we look, we find only a few locations of preserved lake sediments. These areas are isolated to the larger side canyons which probably represent only a minor period of initial lake sediment infilling from the large runoff basins. The Tonto Plateau would be one of the most likely places for sediment preservation. But it is void of any lake sediments, as are the myriad of other likely locations throughout the Canyon.

Also, the presence of lava-dam remnants near the present level of the Colorado River reveals that the Canyon has undergone only negligible erosion and deepening since the time the dams originally formed. The most plausible interpretation is that the lakes were very short-lived, not allowing enough time for complete sediment infilling. Just as the Grand Canyon is a catastrophically flood-formed feature, the lava dams, likewise, were catastrophically formed and eroded features.

SCOTT RUGG

Two, and only two, major episodes of upheaval struck the Grand Canyon.

First, enormous forces were required to tilt the thick package of strata found beneath the Great Unconformity, where the basement rock meets the first sedimentary layer. The apparent landslide deposits of the Sixtymile Formation, the dramatically disturbed bedding of the Shinumo Quartzite, and the emplacement of large igneous dikes, as seen here, all seem to testify that this upheaval did not take place over "long ages," but was instead rapid and catastrophic.

The second major upheaval was the rise of the Kaibab Upwarp, a broad uplifted feature of the Colorado Plateau. The Canyon, in fact, cuts "across the grain" of this upwarp, instead of around it as one would expect. From Desert View overlook, it is clear that the sedimentary layers atop the North Rim are 3,000 feet higher than equivalent strata on Marble Platform. Visitors to Carbon Canyon, the heart of this bent package of layers, are typically awestruck at how the layers look as if they were squeezed like toothpaste (as in the picture on page 32). This second great upheaval, like the first, appears to have formed in an instant, not an age.

No other upheavals in Grand Canyon remotely approach the scale of these two. Some have noted that only two major episodes of upheaval can be found in the Bible; one immediately preceding the Flood of Noah: *"…all the fountains of the great deep burst open, and the floodgates of the sky were opened"* (Genesis 7:11) and one immediately following: *"The mountains rose; the valleys sank down to the place which You established for them"* (Psalm 104:8). Can it be that the rocks and the Word of God agree?

BILL HOESCH

(Above) The apparent landslide deposit of the Sixtymile Formation (Andrew Snelling)

(Left) Diabase dike (arrow), intruded through the Hakatai Shale above Hance Rapid (Keith Swenson)

The presence of cross-beds in the sandstone, and even limestone, layers seen in the Grand Canyon is strong testimony for high energy water transport of these sediments. Studies of sandstones exposed in the Grand Canyon reveal cross-beds produced by high velocity water currents that generated sand waves tens of meters in

Cross-bedding in the massive Coconino Sandstone layer (Tom Vail)

height. The cross-bedded Coconino Sandstone (as seen above) exposed in the Grand Canyon continues across Arizona and New Mexico and its equivalents into Texas, Oklahoma, Colorado, and Kansas. Jointly they cover more than 200,000 square miles and have an estimated volume of 10,000 cubic miles. The cross-beds dip to the south and indicate that the sand came from the north. When one looks for a possible source for this sand to the north, none is readily apparent. A very distant source seems to be required.

Cross-bedding is also seen in the Supai Formation.

The scale of the water catastrophe implied by such formations boggles the mind. Yet numerical calculation demonstrates that when significant areas of the continental surface are flooded, strong water currents with velocities of tens of meters per second spontaneously arise. Such currents are analogous to planetary waves in the atmosphere and are driven by the earth's rotation.

This sort of dramatic global-scale catastrophism documented in these layers implies a distinctively different interpretation of the associated fossil record. Instead of representing an evolutionary sequence, the record reveals a successive destruction of ecological habitats in a global tectonic and hydrologic catastrophe. This understanding readily explains why Darwinian intermediate types are systematically absent from the geological record — the fossil record documents a brief and intense global destruction of life and not a long evolutionary history! The types of plants and animals preserved as fossils were the forms of life that existed on the earth prior to the catastrophe. The long span of time and the intermediate forms of life that the evolutionist imagines in his mind are simply illusions. And the strong observational evidence for the catastrophe absolutely demands a radically revised time scale relative to that assumed by evolutionists.

JOHN BAUMGARDNER

Fossils tell a story, but the story we "read" depends on the "glasses" we are wearing when we do the examination. If we wear our evolutionary glasses during the examination, we will get one story. But if we have on our biblical glasses, which allow us to see biblical truth, we will get a very different story.

Before we start reading their story, it is important to understand just what fossils are and how they are formed. Fossils are the remnants or traces of living things, both plant and animal, found most often in sedimentary rock. In the Grand Canyon, they include everything from the crab-like trilobite, to clams, to worm and reptile tracks, to sea lilies and petrified tree-like ferns, just to name a few.

Fossils are not formed by a plant or animal simply falling to the bottom of an ocean and waiting around for millions of years to be buried. Most scientists would agree that for fossilization to occur, the burial process must be catastrophic in nature. Once a plant or animal is buried in sediment, it is then protected from the elements and turns into rock along with the sediment, but leaving a remnant. This remnant, or fossil, is often coarse but at times can show amazing detail.

So what kind of story do the fossils tell and why is it significant? The first and most significant issue is that fossils represent death! On this, at least, evolutionists and creationists can agree. But, with our biblical glasses on, when does death come into the world? Death is the result of man's sin against God! (Genesis 2:17, 3, Romans 5:12). If fossils are in layers millions of years old, then how do we account for, as Ken Ham would say, "Billions of dead things buried in rock layers laid down by water all over the earth?" How do we justify all the death, disease, and destruction

Trilobite fossil (Gary Parker)

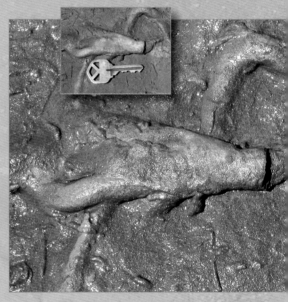

Fossilized worm tracks in the Bright Angel Shale (Tom Vail)

48

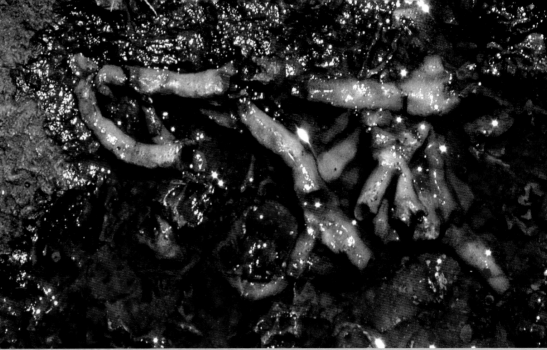

found in the fossil record if those fossils were formed before the Fall?

What else came into the world as a result of sin? Genesis 3:18 says that thorns and thistles were a direct consequence of sin. How do we account for the fossils of thorns found deep within the geologic record, if they are a result of man's sin? If God declared the world as *"very good,"* which He did at the end of creation week, could that have included such things as cancer and arthritis, which we also find in the fossil record? As Dr. Duane Gish's book title says, *Evolution: The Fossils STILL Say No!,* the fossil record does not support the evolutionary story.

If plants and animals have "evolved" slowly over time, why don't we find the intermediate forms of life one would expect in that process? Consider the "evolution" of the automobile. If we visit junkyards around the country, we can find remnants of cars showing the "evolution" from the Model "A" to the modern-day Thunderbird. They would include the intermediate models which tell the evolving story of the automobile, including everything from better alternators to better windshield wipers.

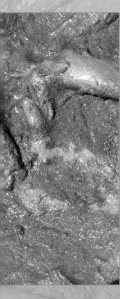

Fossilized worm tubes

But we don't find intermediate forms in the fossil record. We don't find an "almost" clam, or a trilobite showing stages in the development of its very complex eyes. What we do find are fully developed and functional creatures right from their first appearance.

The next few pages will explore some of the fossils found in the Grand Canyon, including one of the largest and maybe the most interesting, the meter-long nautiloid.

Fossilized coral cluster

The first abundant fossil record of complex invertebrates appears in rocks of the so-called Cambrian Period (see diagram on page 36), which is represented in the Grand Canyon by as much as 2,000 feet of the lower sedimentary layers. It is assumed by evolutionists that the sediments which formed the rocks of the Cambrian began to be deposited about 530 million years ago and that the time involved in their deposition stretched over five to ten million years. In Cambrian rocks are found fossils of clams, snails, trilobites, sponges, crinoids, brachiopods, worms, jellyfish, sea urchins, sea cucumbers, swimming crustaceans, sea lilies, and other complex invertebrates. The appearance of this great variety of complex creatures is so startlingly sudden that it is commonly referred to as the "Cambrian explosion" in geological literature.

Sedimentary rocks that are believed to have formed prior to the Cambrian Period are assigned to a rather nebulous period called the Precambrian. Rocks of the Precambrian generally underlie (although not always) Cambrian rocks and are believed to have been laid down during several hundreds of millions of years preceding the Cambrian. There are now many reports in the scientific literature of the discovery in Precambrian rocks of fossils of microscopic, single-celled, soft-bodied creatures, such as bacteria and algae. On the basis of these claims, evolutionists

(Top) Fossilized crinoids (Gary Parker)

(Above) Arrows point out fossils in this small section of Redwall Limestone. (Tom Vail)

are asserting that life arose on earth more than three billion years ago, perhaps as much as three and one-half billion years ago.

If single-celled creatures gave rise to the vast array of complex invertebrates which abruptly burst upon the scene, and nearly three billion years intervened between the origin of life and this "Cambrian explosion" of complicated invertebrates, we must find the record of that evolution somewhere in the rocks of the Precambrian. Ever since Darwin, the rocks have been intensely searched for this record, but to evolutionists the results have been agonizingly disappointing.

Fossilized sea urchin spine, found at South Canyon in Marble Canyon (Joe Pollock)

Nowhere on this earth, neither on any continent nor on the bottom of any ocean, have we been able to find the intermediates between single-celled organisms and the complex invertebrates. Wherever or whenever we find them, right from the start, jellyfish are jellyfish, trilobites are trilobites and sea urchins are sea urchins.

DUANE GISH

51

(Above) Horn corals are seen in the cliffs rising from the river's edge. (Tom Vail)

(Right) Fossilized clam (Gary Parker)

Billions of large fossilized orthocone (cone-shaped) nautiloids are entombed in a six foot thick layer near the base of the massive Redwall Limestone formation. This extraordinary layer persists throughout the Grand Canyon region, northern Arizona and southern Nevada. The fossil bed occupies an area of at least 5,700 square miles and contains an average of one fossilized nautiloid per square yard.

The nautiloids are ancient cephalopods, relatives of the modern-day squid and octopus. Nautiloids were large creatures, with an average shell length of over eighteen inches, with some approaching five feet in length. Nautiloid fossils are observed almost everywhere in the Grand Canyon where good layering surfaces are exposed in this relatively thin bed within the Redwall Limestone.

A gigantic population of these nautiloids appears to have been overcome by a catastrophic event of regional extent, resulting in a mass-kill of an entire population of nautiloids. Orientations of nautiloids indicate they were swept up in a swift westward or southwestward sediment flow. In some locations, as many as 25 percent of the nautiloids are standing perpendicular to the bedding, with the pointed ends downward. These upright nautiloids indicate that rapid sedimentation abruptly captured the shell at various angles. Evidence suggests that these creatures were buried alive very rapidly. That bodies were occupying the shells at the time of burial is implied by the

(Above) Eight-inch cross section of a perpendicular nautiloid

(Left) Artist rendition of a nautiloid

orientation pattern, by shell fragmentation patterns consistent with implosion (violent collapsing or bursting inwards due to rapid compression), and by poor preservation of the shells adjacent to their body cavities.

The sedimentary event that entombed these nautiloids appears to have been a massive sandy debris flow. The base of the debris flow appears to have been a high-density zone, not allowing large, low-density objects like the nautiloids to accumulate. The upper part of the flow appears to have been low-density and turbulent, creating the environment where the nautiloids could be deposited. Sediment quickly amassed to imbed the nautiloids in vertical or inclined orientations.

The existence of the nautiloid fossils in such enormous quantities in such a relatively thin layer that spreads throughout the Canyon area is further evidence that the layers of the Grand Canyon are in fact flood deposits — deposits from a flood of truly catastrophic proportions. Such a flood is described in the Bible, the Flood of Noah's day.

(Above) Fossilized nautiloid (Steve Austin)

(Right) This small nautiloid shows the internal structure of the animal. The shell is divided into chambers by walls (septae) with a central tube (siphuncle) connecting the chambers. The tube allowed depth control by regulating the gas content of each chamber. (Tom Vail)

53

STEVE AUSTIN

Fossilized nautiloids are abundant in a thin layer of the Redwall Limestone.

Fossils are common in the Grand Canyon. From fossils of algal mats in some of the oldest rocks to sponges in the youngest; from footprints of trilobites to footprints of lizards; from a dragonfly wing to a seed fern leaf, there are remains of long-ago living plants and animals of the ocean and land. They belie the beauty and complexity of a world now gone – reflecting the glory and wisdom of the God of Creation. The algal mats were likely from hot-spring-warmed waters far out to sea, and the dragonflies winged their way among seed ferns and scale trees in a continent-sized floating forest. The trilobites swam among sea lilies and bryozoans in broad shallow-water seas.

Most of these animals and plants didn't live here, though. In God's judgment of man's sin, these marvelous communities were destroyed. The animals and plants were carried here from distant locations by powerful currents and quickly buried by sediment. Sea lilies, or crinoids, and bryozoans (right), as seen in the Redwall Limestone for example, were ripped away from their normal moorings and carried here from a great distance. Their broken condition betrays the power of the process and their delicate preservation the rapidity of it all.

God, however, did not totally destroy that original creation, but provided a way that the purified creation could be preserved. Today, plants, animals, and man find their homes in the very earth God judged. Man continues to marvel at the monument God has left. The Grand Canyon is a testimony of our Lord's judgment *and* mercy.

KURT WISE

(Above) *Crinoid stem and bryozoan fossils found in Redwall Cavern* (Keith Swenson)

(Right) *Fossilized fern* (Gary Parker)

54

But Jesus answered, "I tell you, if these [disciples] *become silent, the stones will cry out!"* – Luke 19:40

Layers, as seen from the river, in one of the many side canyons

Noah's flood has left its mark indelibly on, and within, the earth's surface. As we look at the Grand Canyon, we see layer upon layer of rock that contains billions of dead things. As creationist geologists so clearly have pointed out, these layers are not the result of slow processes over millions of years. The evidence from the layers is consistent with their having been laid down catastrophically, by the hydrodynamic action of water — exactly as we would expect from the global Flood of Noah.

KEN HAM

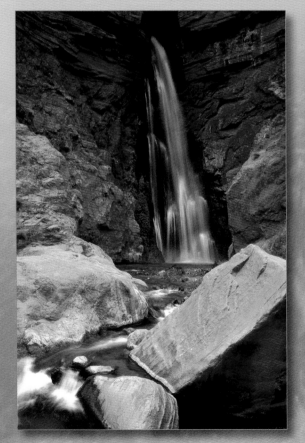

But the falling mountain crumbles away, and the rock moves from its place; water wears away stones, its torrents wash away the dust of the earth . . . – Job 14:18-19

Deer Creek cuts through the layers in the narrows (above) before falling over 100 feet (left) into a pool just yards from the river. (left, courtesy of Arizona River Runners)

No matter what one's worldview, most everyone agrees that the Canyon is a water-carved feature. What we see today is an enormous canyon with a relatively small river running through it; a river that flows at an average of only about four miles per hour, but in places exceeds 25 miles per hour; a river that runs deep and narrow in places and shallow

In the Canyon, what is revealed in God's Word is exactly what one sees. The mountains crumble; the rocks move; the water wears and washes away. In the Canyon, water is a force to be respected. The same water that cools your thirst one minute can become a deluge the next, washing away not only the dust, but the boulders under it.

and wide in others; a river that, prior to man's intervention, would flood each spring, with flows at times reaching over 300,000 cubic feet of water per second and would occasionally trickle down to less than 1,000; a river that is calm and soothing one minute and a raging torrent the next; a river that is considered by many to have some of the biggest and most challenging whitewater in North America.

Since the construction of Glen Canyon Dam in 1963, the Canyon has undergone enormous changes. Spring floods no longer come and wash away the old, to be replaced by the new. The flood waters that removed not only the plants, but the soil as well, no longer thunder though the Canyon. The receding floods no longer leave behind fresh soil for new growth. Because the banks of the Colorado are no longer scoured by spring floods, a new lush riparian life zone has taken hold at the river's edge. As we will see later, this has had a dramatic affect on the entire food chain.

Now the river runs cold, flowing from Glen Canyon Dam at an average of about 48 degrees. The water is too cold to support the spawning of native fish, which have been relegated to spawn in just a few warm side streams. Instead, this cold clear water creates an ideal environment for the introduced rainbow trout.

The riverbed itself is also affected by the lack of spring floods. The pre-dam river would occasionally rise to the task of clearing itself. Debris washed into the river that was not moved downstream by the normal flows, would often be cleared out by the increased velocity of the flood waters.

But the river is not the only source of water in the Grand Canyon. The side

Thunder Springs cascading from the Redwall Limestone (Joe Pollock)

Whispering Springs (Joe Pollock)

streams, as they rush to meet the river, are some of God's grandest displays of the power and the life-sustaining properties of water. As water gushes from the cliffs or trickles from between the rocks, it brings and attracts life. With the harsh desert as their neighbor, the side streams create a lush landscape that is inviting to all. With names like Elves Chasm, Whispering Springs, and Thunder River, they are places to view firsthand the wonders of His handiwork.

From time to time, the true power of water is seen as the sky collapses over the Canyon and funnels the rain into the narrow side canyons. Enormous walls of water and debris roll down the canyons like freight trains. Sometimes carrying as much debris as water, these flows can move house-sized boulders long distances at amazing speeds. It is these flash floods and debris flows that still deepen the side canyons of the Grand Canyon today.

Side canyons are some of the most interesting features of the Grand Canyon. They, too, are erosional remnants. The North Rim of the Canyon is about one thousand feet higher than the South Rim, and the general slope of the land is to the south as well. Therefore, rain that falls on the South Rim flows away from the Canyon. But rain that falls on the North Rim flows into the Canyon, eroding the rim back as the water rushes to the river. The result is, in general, that the side canyons on the North Rim stretch back farther from the river than those on the South Rim.

(Above) Clear Creek Falls (Chuck Hill)

(Right) The challenging climb into Silver Grotto is rewarded by extraordinary evidence for the power of water.

58

Although many of the side canyons are very large, extending back miles from the river, the majority are relatively shallow amphitheaters or "C-shaped" features. The

Note the example of small-scale sapping in the sand at the river's edge.

question is: how did they get their start in the first place? They are primarily the product of a process called "sapping." As material is laid down in a watery environment, such as a flood, the material is saturated with water. As long as the water table is above the material, the water remains "trapped" there. But once the water table drops, as with a receding flood, the trapped water starts to escape. As the water from the lower part of the structure seeps out of the sediment, the structure weakens, causing a collapse of the material above, resulting in an amphitheater-shaped canyon. This same sapping process can often be

Lower Stone Creek Falls (Jacque Kewalramani)

seen today in the sand banks along the Colorado River, although on a much smaller scale.

As we travel the Canyon's length, we see literally hundreds of these amphitheaters along the rim, which is exactly what we would predict from water-soaked sediment after the receding of a massive catastrophic event like Noah's flood.

As you enjoy the water-related features shown here, remember that this same water was once used for another purpose, to judge and forever change the world in which we live.

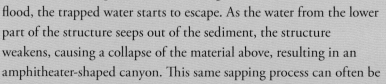

He sends forth springs in the valleys; they flow between the mountains . . . — Psalm 104:10

The Grand Canyon, because of its size and depth, can create its own weather. Winds flow up and down the Canyon and over the edge as storms and the sun interact with the steep walls. The results range from 15 feet of snow on the North Rim in the winter to 120-degree temperatures at river level in the summer.

If it rains while you are in the Canyon, you may be blessed with a light, gentle drizzle. But in the summer, you are more likely to experience thunderstorms, which can dump an inch of rain in less than an hour. Thunderstorms can turn the Canyon's streams into muddy torrents pouring from every gully and cliff. Rain does not soak into the ground, but runs off all of the rocky surfaces almost as soon as it falls. Small gullies can become streams, small streams rivers, and rivers a torrent. It is awe inspiring to watch water falling in sheets and waves from the cliffs surrounding you. The noise of large raindrops hitting the ground, water splashing from cliffs above, and thunder echoing among the side canyons can be intimidating.

When the rain ends and the water stops flowing a few minutes later, you might think you are in heaven. If it's late in the afternoon, brilliant rainbows break out toward the east. The fresh smell of soil and sage after a rain permeates the air, and the sound of the canyon wren signals a fresh start. This must have been something like what Noah experienced after the Flood.

LARRY VARDIMAN

(Above) Spectacular and seldom-seen runoff, the result of a summer thunderstorm over Marble Canyon (Tom Vail)

(Background) Rainbow in the eastern sky

(Far Right) View upstream from The Tabernacle of an approaching thunderstorm

Listen closely to the thunder of His voice . . . – Job 37:2

Where did the Grand Canyon itself come from? The Flood may have stacked the rock like a giant layer cake, but what cut the cake? One thing is sure: the Colorado River did not do it. The river starts about 12,000 feet up in the Rocky Mountains of western Colorado. By the time it gets to the head of the Grand Canyon, it's at an elevation of only 3,000 feet or so. And that is the problem. The Grand Canyon is definitely not a lowland valley. The North Rim of the Canyon is

over 8,000 feet high! For the Colorado River to carve the Canyon, it would first have had to hack its way almost a mile uphill! Water just doesn't do that, especially when there is the opportunity to flow downhill in a different direction.

GARY PARKER

Downstream view of Lava Falls, from Toroweap Overlook

Travertine is generally formed in waters saturated with calcium carbonate which has been dissolved as water flows though limestone formations. The calcium carbonate is then "redeposited" to form the travertine. Formations can develop very quickly, as seen on the twig below that was submerged in the flowing waters of Havasu Creek for a matter of months. Cascading dams are formed over hundreds of years, not millions, only to later be washed away by the monsoon floods. The remnant of one of those dams is seen at bottom.

Travertine Falls (Joe Pollock)

63

Travertine on a stick
(Tom Vail)

Travertine dam remnant (Tom Vail)

Havasu Canyon, with its magnificent waterfalls, is one of the true jewels of the Grand Canyon. The Havasupai Indians have lived in this remote canyon for centuries. It is accessible only by foot, horse, and now, helicopter. "Havasu" is a Havasupai word which is most commonly translated "blue-green waters," and a captivating blue-green creek it is.

Havasu Creek is fed from springs that flow through limestone formations which saturate the water with dissolved calcium carbonate. The calcium carbonate coats the bottom of the creek and reflects the sky, creating the majestic color of the water. It is that same calcium carbonate that coats everything left in the water for more than a few days with a layer of travertine. Often large pools are created as the travertine builds up to form dams that seem to almost dance in the sunlight as the water cascades over them.

The serenity of Havasu Canyon (Chuck Hill)

(Above) View of Beaver Falls from the trail

(Right) Cascading blue-green pools of Havasu Creek

(Left) Mooney Falls in Havasu Canyon, at 190 feet, is higher than Niagara Falls.

Thunderstorms, with their loud peals of thunder and lightning snaking across the sky, are impressive events that remind us of the power and majesty of God. Normally thunderstorms occur in the Grand Canyon area during the late summer. The rain is so heavy

*For just
as the lightning
comes from the east
and flashes even to the west, so
will the coming of the Son of Man be.*

– Matthew 24:27

Cloud-to-ground lightning in a summer thunderstorm

at times that it causes flash floods. Dirt and rocks can be eroded by the rushing water, causing a debris flow. Occasionally, enough debris rushes out of a side canyon and spills into the Colorado River to raise the river level and sometimes temporarily blocking it. The vast majority of the rapids found in the Grand Canyon are the result of these debris flows.

These events can cause a person to wonder whether thunderstorms, as well as other rainstorms and snowmelt, could have contributed to the origin of the Grand Canyon. Most uniformitarian thinkers, those who believe that physical processes have operated in essentially the same way through time, are convinced that the erosion and deposition we see today has, over a period of millions of years, formed the Canyon. There are several uniformitarian hypotheses that use water and long periods of time to explain the formation of the Canyon. However, recently dated sedimentary rocks just west of the Grand Canyon have forced some evolutionary scientists to postulate that the Canyon formed quickly sometime between one and six million years ago. If the Canyon formed rapidly, processes observed today, such as gully-washing thunderstorms, seem less likely to have played a major role in carving the Grand Canyon and its side canyons. A catastrophic mechanism for the formation of the Grand Canyon seems more likely, even within the evolutionary model. Within the creation framework, the Grand Canyon originated only several thousand years ago as a direct or indirect result of Noah's flood. So we would expect that thunderstorms and flash floods would have had no effect on the Canyon's original formation.

Thunderstorms and their resulting rain have, however, slightly widened and possibly deepened the Grand Canyon since its formation. Besides debris flows, another known effect of thunderstorms is that they recharge the water table near the top of the Canyon, which contributes to the sapping process that forms the ubiquitous amphitheaters.

The Grand Canyon must have been originally formed by catastrophic processes. Present processes, including thunderstorms, do not provide a satisfactory explanation for its origin, but have merely modified its width and depth slightly.

MIKE OARD

(Right) Marble Canyon and the North Rim, from Eminence Break Trail

(Below) Much of the electrical energy of a thunderstorm dissipates within the clouds in what is called cloud-to-cloud lightning.

Life at the Grand Canyon ranges from the bluebird that frequents the spruce and fir forests of the North Rim to the endangered humpback chub that struggles for survival in the unnaturally cold waters of the Colorado River. What we see in this sometimes harsh environment is clear evidence of the intelligent design of our Creator. As we observe the natural community around us, it becomes obvious that there is an intelligence built into the flora and fauna eking out a living there.

Within the four life zones of the Grand Canyon, those "zones" defined by the plants and animals that live in them, most creatures live a relatively peaceful existence. The eagles soar overhead, the snakes and lizards sun themselves on the rocks, while the harvest ants

Pricklypear cactus in bloom (Joe Pollock)

Desert bighorn sheep
(Tom Vail)

scurry around cleaning the beaches. It is true, however, since we live in a fallen world, that if you are the ant, you don't want to see the lizard coming, and if you're the lizard, you don't want to find yourself in the path of the snake, just as the snake wants to avoid being caught in the shadow of the eagle.

Interdependency is a common theme, especially in plant-animal relationships. For example, the flower of the lupine requires the weight of the honey bee to expose its pollen, which the bee then transports to the next flower. The flower of the yucca can only be fertilized by the yucca moth, which in turn lays its eggs in the flower. Then, once the eggs hatch, the seed of the yucca becomes food for the moth's larvae. And as the nocturnal sphinx moth feeds with its long proboscis, it is responsible for pollinating the sacred datura, a night-blooming member of the nightshade family.

Evidence of the Creator's design is also readily seen throughout the plant and animal community. For example, the plants that are

Ocotillo along the path to Havasu Creek

Fishhook cactus (Tom Vail)

native to the inner depths of the Canyon, such as the yellow-flowering brittlebush, distribute themselves across the terrain in a manner that allows each to collect enough water to survive. Is this a strategy that has developed by chance over millions of years? Have these plants "learned" to grow this way, or is this a strategy of design? The ocotillo, which is not a cactus though it has thorns like one, has the ability to conserve water by dropping its leaves, giving it the appearance of being dead. But within three to four days after rain falls, it is again covered with a coat of bright green leaves.

The influence of man is witnessed in the Canyon, especially in the riparian zone along the river's edge, a zone that has been dramatically altered by the "control" of the river by Glen Canyon Dam. It is quite different from what existed along the pre-dam river. Prior to the dam, the riparian zone was sparsely vegetated due to the annual scouring by spring floods. The man-altered environment along the river is now overgrown with a variety of native and non-native plants. This expanded band of vegetation has created more habitats for bugs, which attracts more lizards, which in turn attracts more birds, and right on up the food chain.

This "new" riparian zone does not represent evolution, since plants and animals are not changing but rather opportunistically migrating into a new ecosystem. No new life forms are seen in this new environment, just ants tunneling in the sand, lizards scurrying around in the shade of vegetation no longer scoured by the floods, and birds nesting in the trees which thrive in the water provided by the river. We also see mule deer

The sphinx moth both feeds on and pollinates the sacred datura.

and an array of birds now living along the river where adequate food and shelter did not exist in the pre-dam environment.

Glen Canyon Dam has modified the aquatic ecosystem as well. The once warm autumn waters of the Colorado were the spawning ground for a variety of native fish. But the dam reduced the water temperature by as much as 30 degrees, making it inhospitable to native fish. Introduced trout now thrive in the clear cold water, while most of the native fish are either extinct or endangered. For example, only a few thousand of the odd-shaped humpback chub remain in Grand Canyon.

Evidence of the Fall is also obvious in the Grand Canyon's plant life, particularly at the lower elevations. Thorns and thistles, which are a direct result of the curse (Genesis 3:18), are plentiful

Juvenile Red-spotted toad, shown life-size (Tom Vail)

There are three things which are too wonderful for me, four which I do not understand: the way of an eagle in the sky, the way of a serpent on a rock . . .

– Proverbs 30:18-19

(Above left) Cardinal monkey-flower, found along Tapeats Creek

(Left) Grand Canyon rattlesnake

and are waiting along every trail, eager to make their presence felt. The Canyon magnificently displays God's created plants and animals. Design is apparent everywhere if you are willing to look and investigate with a receptive mind. Open your eyes and mind to the world around you and you will quickly see the beauty and complexity of His designs, not just in the Grand Canyon but in your own back yard as well.

(Above) A western collared lizard standing tall for a different view

(Left) Monkey-faced spider (David Toney)

(Right) Century plant in bloom

The endangered humpback chub will sometimes find the fisherman's lure but is quickly released. (Joe Pollock)

To the mind's eye, the great spectacle of the Grand Canyon is a series of snap shots that sums up the experiences of standing quietly at select vantage points on the rim, along the trails, on the river's bank, or anywhere that one takes a breather to embrace God's silent "Fourth of July" celebration. For the grandeur is in the moment

and setting. Although there is hardly any Canyon viewpoint that doesn't take effort and time to reach, the reward is the personal reflection of what is seen that strokes one's memory into existence.

Today's visitors predominantly arrive at the South Rim among the ponderosa pine parklands. It is pleasant to walk through the towering pines and Gambel oak, under-laced by cliff rose, fernbush, and sagebrush. As you stride along dirt or duff paths experiencing the morning or evening coolness, the Steller's jay and Abert squirrels chatter above.

Hiking is the best means to capture the memories. Whether by rim walks or trail descents, you have to hoof it and frequently scramble over the rock formations to get that next shot. The Park has two principal botanical displays to offer – horizontal mature or elfin forests and vertical stratified plant communities. Because the South Rim is at the 7,000-foot elevation, there is a cool, moist climate that sustains the mature forest. However, once you start down a trail into the abyss, you travel successively through four regions of increasing heat and dryness.

Leaving the stately ponderosas, the next layer is about 2,000 feet thick, consisting mostly of pinyon pine and Utah juniper. Pinyons are small trees with short, bushy needles and delicious cone nuts. The junipers rely on their scales to accommodate the drier conditions. Within this community, rock squirrels and mule deer graze. An understory of big sagebrush, rabbitbrush, and snakeweed make for a fairly dense low-form forest overlaying the uppermost rock layers

(Above left) Hopi Point
(David Toney)

(Right) Narrowleaf yucca
(David Toney)

View from South Kaibab Trail above Skeleton Point
(David Toney)

of the Canyon. As you move down below the Redwall cliffs, an extensive elfin forest of black brush scrub coats the broad plateaus. Narrowleaf yucca, beavertail and hedgehog cactus, and Mormon tea are interspersed.

Springs emerge from the cliff walls and feed small creeks that cascade through the rocks on their way to the river below. Along their courses, riparian sedges, reeds, algae, grasses, and enormous cottonwood trees can be found. A spectacular burst of color is seen in the enormous bouquet of a western redbud tree in the spring. It is along these watery corridors that you may encounter the black-chinned hummingbird, hooded oriole, or even the endangered willow flycatcher.

Finally, a sparse, prickly community of desert scrub covers the terraces and talus slopes of the inner gorge. Mesquite, four-wing saltbush, ocotillo, and century-plant inhabit the shaley debris. This very dry terrain abruptly abuts the cold, rushing Colorado River. Water is abundant and turbulent in the channel, but its reach into the water table of the beach is short, extending only a short distance from the shoreline. There, lacey tamarisk trees bloom and send billows of cottony seeds upstream in the northeasterly flowing winds. Coyote willow, arrow weed and desert broom thrive along the river's edge.

In all communities, there are intermittent showy displays of annual and perennial flowers. Evening primrose is a welcome gift; sacred datura, with its huge trumpet blossoms on winding vines, is a short-lived surprise; asters, fleabane, and golden columbine show up unannounced; yellow and red cardinal monkey-flower are seen at places where water seeps from the Canyon wall; penstemon, carmine thistle, shooting stars, and an array of cacti all have their places and times of flowering.

73

Beavertail cactus (David Toney)

In the Canyon, rocks rule the horizons but plants ease the harshness. Both are relics of cataclysmic happenings long ago. Very little has changed since those events; still, seasonal parades of birth, growth, and decay offer infinite memories for the eye of the soul.

KEN CUMMING

In the cold, clear, algal green waters of the Colorado, along the river's banks and hiking trails, streambeds, and crevasses in the Canyon's Inner Gorge, you will meet several fascinating animals. They all challenge evolutionary belief, supporting instead what the Bible tells us about Earth's history.

Manmade dams block the mad rush of warm, turbid, reddish water and seasonal flooding, replacing it with clear, cold, only slightly pulsating flow released from deep below the reservoir's surface. You will see fishermen angling for exotic rainbow trout that quickly replaced the pre-dam species — but you will not see any evidence that the earlier species evolved from some other kind of fish in response to these changed conditions.

Without severe seasonal floods to scour the river banks clean, plants colonized the sandbars along the river's edge, with animals quickly following their lead. This simple-to-complex development from a bare mineral environment (open sandbars) to diverse biotic communities is called ecological succession, not evolution. It is based on migration, not mutation – animals moving from one environment to another as conditions change, not animals changing from one kind to another.

Among the animals colonizing the river's edge and extending up into the stream-side riparian habitats, look for birds like the American avocet or snowy egret along the river's bank; the awesome great blue heron fishing in quiet backwaters; visiting mallard ducks paddling in open water. Listen for the tiny Lucy's warbler among the willows and tamarisk or the canyon wren as it flits among the rocks. The amphibians you may catch a glimpse of include the canyon treefrog and red-spotted toad and their offspring tadpoles. Dragonflies dart about overhead while aquatic larvae scavenge the streambeds for food. The Grand Canyon rattlesnake and side-blotched lizard represent the reptiles. Mammals often seen include the ring-tailed cat, spotted skunk, mule deer, bighorn sheep, and the occasional coyote.

(Above) Mule deer now live along the river.

(Left) The four-foot great blue heron is dwarfed by the Canyon walls.

Canyon treefrog (Tom Vail)

In hikes to higher, drier environments that can be extremely hot in the daytime sun, you'll see animals with exquisite design features (adaptations) that make them as comfortably at home in the desert as we are in air-conditioned houses, sipping a cold drink. By moving in and out of the shade and changing body angle with respect to the sun, the aptly named collared lizard and the chunky chuckwalla lizard maintain proper body temperature behaviorally as easily as we do physiologically. Both we and the kangaroo rat can manufacture "metabolic water" from eating dry seeds, but the kangaroo rat produces urine so concentrated and feces so dense it never needs to drink! You may also see a jackrabbit sitting in the shade with its big ears fully extended, not for hearing, but to radiate surplus heat.

Animals you will not see down near the river are the tassel-eared squirrels that live in the cool pine forests on the North and South Rims, the Kaibab and Abert squirrels, respectively. Despite the awesome chasm that separates them, traits of these two populations grade evenly into one another, proving their separation could not have been long. Thus, those squirrels act as "biological clocks" telling us the Canyon formed rapidly and recently, pointing away from evolution and toward the truth of God's Word!

75

(Above) American avocets (Tom Vail)

(Left) Curious ringtail cat

GARY PARKER

Rock nettle (Tom Vail)

The rock nettle, with its harsh, hair-like stickers, is likely a direct result of the curse.

Ravens (Tom Vail)

Ravens are fascinating birds. Often called the "geniuses of the bird world," they are curious and mischievous. They mate for life and live happily ever after in their own territory. They share the responsibilities of raising their family, and the young share the territory with their parents while they grow and learn. The male provides and protects, while the female is his helpmate. In times of adversity or danger, male and female work as a team to overcome it. Ravens, by God-given instinct, faithfully live out life much like God's Word tells us we should live.

ighorn sheep frequent the river corridor to graze, especially during the summer when water sources are less abundant in the higher regions. A large ram (male) will reach a height of five and a half feet with the ewes (female) standing about a foot shorter. Rams live alone or in small groups, while the ewes tend to live in small herds of six to twenty.

In the fall, the rams "fight" for the mating rights to a group of ewes and then aggressively defend their herd. Females birth one or two young in early spring that will stay with the herd for two or more years.

The ram's massive horns will reach a full curl in about seven years but the ends may be intentionally rubbed off on rocks if they start to block their peripheral vision. The horns of the female are shorter with less curl.

The sheep are as comfortable on the steep rock faces as on flat ground. (Tom Vail)

Protective camouflage blends sheep into their surroundings, allowing the females to wait in the shade for the midday heat to pass.

On the cliff face to the right is a baby sheep separated from his mother (see enlargements). Can you find them? — See next page for locations. *(Tom Vail)*

Adult males develop a fully curled horn in about seven years. *(Tom Vail)*

. . . And He set my feet upon a rock making my footsteps firm . . . — Psalm 40:2

A white desert bighorn sheep wandering in a brown desert environment? Doesn't seem to make sense. Even the other sheep seem to wonder about him. What happened here?

Obviously this is a mistake, a genetic copying mistake known as a mutation. Something was lost or corrupted in the reproductive process that should have provided this sheep with the information to develop the "normal" camouflaged coat — one that permits bighorn sheep to virtually disappear among the rocks. In a truly natural environment with its natural predators, this sheep likely would not have lasted through its first year.

Even the normal-colored sheep seem to wonder about the white sheep. (Tom Vail)

It was a loss of information that flawed this sheep, which would have had a better chance of success in the snow. Had it lived successfully in a snowy environment, it would have passed on the mutated gene to its offspring, which in turn would have had a better chance of survival. That is an inherited biological change. Many insist on calling all such changes "evolution," but such adaptive change *within a kind* is always the result of a loss of information, not an increase.

Molecules-to-man evolution requires mutations that produce additional (new) information in order to be able to support the idea of lizards sprouting feathers and taking to flight. If the biological changes we see around us were a small part of this process, then we would expect to see many examples of an increase in genetic information. But we don't.

The Bible teaches that animals were made "after their kind." Genesis 1:25 says, *"God made the beasts of the earth after their kind, and the cattle after their kind, and everything that creeps on the ground after its kind…"* Nowhere in nature, the fossil record, or the laboratory, do we see any inherited changes that are informationally "uphill." What we see is sheep remaining sheep, sometimes with less information than their parents, but they are still just sheep.

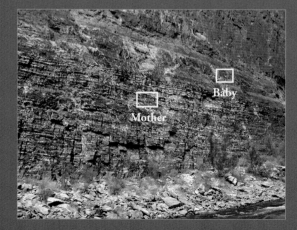

Mother

Baby

Location of mother and baby sheep from previous page

Dragonflies, as they dart along the river's edge and up the side streams, are among the most striking forms of insects. But even more amazing is their spectacular flight. They have a completely different principle for flying than any other of the 800,000 insects. Most insects' flight is controlled by muscles in the thorax area which push the wing up when tightened and down when relaxed. In contrast, the dragonfly has muscles connected directly to the wing joints by tendons, allowing them to be the only true acrobatic fliers. Their design is the forerunner to the modern-day helicopter. Pioneer helicopter designer Igor Sikorsky got the idea for the development of the helicopter from his observations of the dragonfly.

The dragonfly's legs are designed for catching instead of walking. They can be opened during flight to form a "catcher" to snatch their prey out of the air. Their eyes, comprising the majority of the head surface, are made up of up to 30,000 six-sided individual eyes. They "see" through rapid sequential bursts of light, up to 200 per second, which are individually registered, creating an image that is similar to that produced by a television camera.

These, along with many other unique design features of the dragonfly, show the Creator's richness of invention and His love for beauty. So we shouldn't be surprised by their beauty and glorious design, since we come from the same Creator's workshop.

WERNER GITT

81

otanist George W. Vasey never visited the Canyon and therefore never saw his "paradise." The title was bestowed by Grand Canyon explorer Major John Wesley Powell, who on August 9, 1869, described a "wall set with a million brilliant gems" and "fountains bursting from the rock high overhead." Powell named this patch of verdant spring-fed greenery "Vasey's Paradise," after his botanist friend who had traveled through the Rocky Mountains with him the year before.

Vasey's Paradise is a haven of botanical diversity harboring orchids, crimson monkeyflowers, redbud trees, maidenhair ferns, lush beds of watercress and even poison ivy. It contrasts sharply with the adjacent barren Redwall Limestone and serves as a visual reminder that plants (and all organisms) need water and that where water is plentiful, life abounds. Following the catastrophic carving of Grand and Marble Canyons, the newly formed landscape would have appeared devoid of life. But over the ensuing months, years, and decades, surviving organisms, as well as immigrant species from more distant sites, populated this place. One of the major determinants of the rate and character of that recovery was the presence (or absence) of water.

The cardinal monkey-flower, with its bright green foliage and even brighter red flower, is found along many side streams. (Tom Vail)

For with Thee is the fountain of life . . . – Psalm 36:9

Lower Ribbon Falls (David Toney)

In a similar way, but on a much grander scale, earth's entire biosphere once rebounded following a global cataclysmic disturbance – the Flood in the days of Noah. The products of that reclamation include the forests, tundra, savannas, prairies, and deserts which we see on the modern earth – each a testimony to the life-giving power of water and the incredible resilience built into the flora and fauna by its Creator.

KEITH SWENSON

He brought forth streams also from the rock and caused waters to run down like rivers. – Psalm 78:16

(Above) Springs supply the life-giving water to Vasey's Paradise.
(Keith Swenson)

(Left) Golden columbine
(Joe Pollock)

Great are the

works of the Lord …

Splendid and majestic is

His work … He has made His

wonders to be remembered …

– Psalm 111:2-4

Deer Creek Narrows

The brittle bush provides a blanket of yellow in spring, but is dormant by mid-summer.

(Series by Joe Pollock)

He waters the mountains from His upper chambers; the earth is satisfied with the fruit of His works. – Psalm 104:13

GRAND CANYON

THE "BEDROCK"

S ee to it that no one takes you captive through philosophy and empty deception, according to the tradition of men, according to the elementary principles of the world, rather than according to Christ. – Colossians 2:8

As you travel through the Canyon, you will eventually reach "bedrock," that point where you can go down no farther. It is when you reach this point that you find the biggest and most challenging rapids. Your travel through life is much the same — at some point the only way to look is up.

Most people look at the Canyon with some preconceived ideas on how it was formed. Those ideas are generally based on their background, which is foundational to their worldview – the bedrock of their belief system. I challenge you, if you have not already done so, to set your worldview aside and consider the evidence given here with an open mind.

The Bible encourages us to evaluate everything for ourselves. 1 Thessalonians 5:21 says, *"But examine everything carefully; hold fast to that which is good . . ."*

How great are Your works, O Lord! Your thoughts are very deep. – Psalm 92:5

Depths of the lower Canyon

Don't accept what you hear or read as truth without evaluating the facts for yourselves, including what you have read here.

As an example, consider the story of the Scablands and the "Spokane Flood." The Scablands are a 15,000 square mile area of eastern Washington of deeply gouged canyons, initially thought to be the product of slow gradual erosion. In 1927, J Harlen Bretz presented a paper to the Geological Society of America suggesting that the Scablands were eroded catastrophically. For 30 years, Bretz was ridiculed for his theory. In 1956, additional information was presented by J. T. Pardee supporting Bretz's theory. Since that time, evidence has been pieced together to show that the Scablands were catastrophically eroded by the "Spokane Flood," which was the result of the failure of an ice dam that had created Lake Missoula. The United States Geological Society (USGS) estimates that the flood released 500 cubic miles of water which drained in as little as 48 hours, gouging out millions of tons of solid rock. In 1979, Bretz was awarded the Penrose Medal, one of geology's highest honors, for his work. Someday that award may go to someone for the discovery that the Grand Canyon also was the result of a single catastrophic event — maybe even a global flood.

Contact between the Coconino Sandstone and the Toroweap Limestone (Tom Vail)

Looking up from the bedrock in Blacktail Canyon (Keith Swenson)

Contrary to the words and theories of man, the Word of God does not change. God does not lie and neither does His Word. Nothing in the Bible has ever been proven to be in error. Time after time, man has questioned the validity of God's Word, yet time after time God's Word has held true, including those areas that touch on science.

Consider just one fact about the Grand Canyon. There is virtually no physical erosion or chemical weathering between many of the sedimentary layers, as seen in the picture to the left. These layers are essentially horizontal across the entire Colorado Plateau. How can this be? Evolutionists would have us believe that these layers were deposited by multiple oceans as a result of the entire Colorado Plateau being raised and lowered, perhaps as many as seven times. They would say the surface of each layer was exposed for millions of years before the next layer was deposited. Yet that exposed surface remained as flat as a pancake. Does this seem logical? Have you ever seen vast areas of totally featureless terrain? These layers are, however, exactly what we would expect to see as the result of a global flood.

Have you read to this point and still say, "This is all foolishness?" Well, that too is predicted in the Bible. 2 Timothy 4:3-4 says, *"For the time will come when they will not endure sound doctrine; but wanting to have their ears tickled, they will accumulate for themselves teachers in accordance to their own desires, and will turn away their ears from the truth and will turn aside to myths."* And 1 Corinthians 1:18 says, *"For the message of the cross* [belief that Jesus Christ died for our sins] *is foolishness to those who are perishing* [not having accepted Jesus Christ as their Lord and Savior]*, but to us who are being saved* [believing in Jesus Christ] *it is the power of God."* Are your ears being tickled?

It's really very simple. It comes down to which book you put your faith in...your college textbook, written by man, or the Bible, written by an omniscient, loving God, a God that sent His only Son to die on the cross for your sins.

As you enjoy the images on the next few pages, consider also the words of God that accompany them, words that plainly warn us of the ways of the world, which attempt to deny the existence of God by taking us *"captive through philosophy and empty deceit, according to the tradition of men, according to the elementary principles of the world, rather than according to Christ"* (Colossians 2:8).

Light dances in Conquistador Aisle, Grand Canyon (Chuck Hill)

And God saw that the light was good; and God separated the light from the darkness. – Genesis 1:4

Rock formations can be spectacularly beautiful. So it's not surprising to find them featured in books and other items in Christian bookstores. A coffee table book or calendar might have a Grand Canyon picture accompanied by, say, *"The everlasting God, the LORD, the Creator of the ends of the earth…"* (Isaiah 40:28). Animal photos, like that of the bighorn sheep shown here along the river's edge, often carry such "creation" passages as well.

The take-home message is clearly meant to be, "God made this" — whether canyon or sheep. In one sense, however, things are not that simple.

The Bible clearly teaches that the heavens, the Earth, and *all* they contain were made during the six days of creation week (*"For in six days the Lord made the heavens and the earth, the sea and all that is in them, and rested on the seventh day…"* Exodus 20:11). But the sheep in the photo was obviously not made then, although the first representatives of its ancestral kind were. The infinitely intelligent Designer constructed their highly complex biology, including the programmed molecular machinery by which they were to "multiply and fill the Earth" — i.e. reproduce — "after their kinds." Today's sheep is the eventual consequence of that original creative act. In fact, it only contains a subset of the information of its ancestral kind, marred by accumulated genetic copying mistakes (mutations).

Bighorn sheep (Tom Vail)

The Canyon, too, is the consequence of the "natural" process of fluids eroding rock. God did not "make" it in the sense of the other things made in creation week. In any case, whatever geological structures were created in those sensational six days, the massive power of the Genesis Flood (and associated catastrophes such as those brought on by the subsequent Ice Age) would have destroyed them.

That's obvious from just looking at the mile-deep sediments, containing trillions of dead things, found not only in the Canyon, but all over the world.

Today's canyons, including the Grand Canyon, are the consequences, not so much of God's creative design, but of the forces He unleashed in divine judgment on sin. So when we contemplate the Canyon's awesome beauty, a simplistic "God made this" is really inadequate. In fact, everything around us is not the world which God made, or at least not the way He first made it. Whether geological or biological, all aspects of it have been marred by a real, historical curse on all creation (Genesis 3, Romans 8:19-22). This universal change came about because of a real, historical rebellion by a real, historical man, Adam. And because of this, God sent His real, historical Son, the Lord Jesus Christ, into the real world of space and time, to bear our sins on the Cross. That's the real take-home message, whether of the sheep or the Canyon.

CARL WIELAND

For they exchanged the truth of God for a lie, and worshiped and served the creature rather than the Creator . . . – Romans 1:25

He who believes in Me, as the Scripture said, "from his innermost being will flow rivers of living water." – John 7:38

Ribbon Falls (David Toney)

What we believe about creation, what we believe about Genesis has implications all the way to the end of Scripture, implications with regard to the veracity and truthfulness of Scripture, implications as to the gospel and implications as to the end of human history all wrapped up in how we understand origins in the book of Genesis. The matter of origins then is absolutely critical to all human thinking. It becomes critical to how we conduct our lives as human beings. Without an understanding of origins, without a right understanding of origins, there is no way to comprehend ourselves. There is no way to understand humanity as to the purpose of our existence, and as to our destiny. If we cannot believe what Genesis says about origins, we are lost as to our purpose and our destiny. Whether this world and its life as we know it evolved by chance, without a cause, or was created by God has immense comprehensive implications for all of human life.

Genesis 1:1 says, "In the beginning God created the heavens and the earth." I don't know how it could be said any more simply or more straightforwardly than that. Either you believe God did create the heavens and the earth or you believe He did not. Really those are the only two valid options you have. And if you believe that God did create the heavens and the earth, then you are left with the only record of that creation and that's Genesis 1 and you are bound to accept the text of Genesis 1 as the only appropriate and accurate description of that creative act.

If you don't believe the book of Genesis, then you are left with the incredible notion that nobody times nothing equals everything.

JOHN MACARTHUR

The Grand Canyon is one of the greatest memorials of God's work that we possess. If only the Christian church took God at His Word, it could be used as one of the great reminders of His power. The evidence for a catastrophic Flood judgment as seen in the Grand Canyon is unmistakable and overwhelming. The evidence is crying out at us—the very stones are crying out! We read in Job, *"… speak to the earth, and let it teach you…"* (Job 12:8).

KEN HAM

Know this first of all, that in the last days mockers will come with their mocking, following after their own lusts, and saying, "Where is the promise of His coming? For ever since the fathers fell asleep, all continues just as it was from the beginning of creation." For when they maintain this, it escapes their notice that by the word of God the heavens existed long ago and the earth was formed out of water and by water, through which the world at that time was destroyed, being flooded with water. – 2 Peter 3:3-6

Lower stretches of Marble Canyon

Some may question using the Bible as a science and/or history book. It is true that it is not a textbook; however, in every area it addresses, as man has learned more about the world around us, the Bible has proven correct in every detail to which it speaks.

Before man understood the water cycle — the evaporation of the oceans causing the formation of clouds, rain from the clouds feeding the rivers, and the water returning once again to the oceans — God said, *"…He who calls for the waters of the sea and pours them out on the face of the earth, the Lord is His name"* (Amos 9:6), and *"All the rivers flow into the sea, yet the sea is not full. To the place where the rivers flow, there they flow again"* (Ecclesiastes 1:7).

While the jet stream and movements of the winds were yet unknown to man, God said, *"Blowing toward the south, then turning toward the north, the wind continues swirling along; and on its circular courses the wind returns"* (Ecclesiastes 1:6).

There are verses that speak to the First and Second Laws of Thermodynamics, atomic structure, oceanography, dinosaurs, medicine, and astronomy. In the book of Job alone, over twenty scientific concepts have been identified.

Many great scientists, like Louis Pasteur, Isaac Newton, and Robert Boyle, were Bible-believing creationists. Matthew Maury, who wrote the first textbook on modern oceanography, based his research on what he read in Psalm 8:8, *"…whatever passes through the paths of the seas."* From information drawn from drift bottles thrown into the seas and washed ashore, he was able to develop charts of the ocean currents, the "paths" of the seas.

The Bible teaches that God existed before the world. *"In the beginning God created the heavens and the earth."* (Genesis 1:1). And God will be here when the world ceases to exist. *"I am the Alpha and the Omega, the first and the last, the beginning and the end"* (Revelation 22:13).

Who better to write the instruction manual on life and the real history of the universe, than God — He created it all. The Bible warns that man will reject the knowledge of God (2 Timothy 4:3-4, Colossians 2:8). This is why man's theories of how the Canyon was formed tend to deny God's involvement. Man's theories continually change as more scientific "facts" come to light. Yet, God has never had to revise His book, because in it, there are no mistakes. There may be some concepts which we do not yet fully understand, but I believe, as always in the past, time will eventually prove them to be true. You can trust God's Word.

PAULA VAIL

. . . I am the light of the world; he who follows Me shall not walk in the darkness . . . – John 8:12

Morning at Yavapai Point, South Rim (David Toney)

94

95

Let's go boatin'! is the call that echoes off the walls of the Grand Canyon during my guided tours. It gets people moving and ready to head down river. In my years as a guide, I've had the privilege of taking thousands of people through the Grand Canyon, through what I now believe to be one of God's true, created wonders.

My love for the Grand Canyon started in 1980 when I went on my first river trip. The following year, I started working as a part-time guide and in 1983, I left my corporate life to work in the Canyon.

For the first 15 years of my career, I thought that evolution was responsible for "forming" the Canyon – millions of years of particle-by-particle deposition, interspersed by long periods of erosion. The profound significance of the Canyon was not yet engraved on my heart. I was being prepared, though, for a major shift in thinking.

One day in July 1994, a lady got off a plane at Marble Canyon, Arizona. She was going on a Grand Canyon rafting trip, and I was one of her guides. Little did I know how much she would be guiding me. My worldview was about to be turned upside-down.

If we had not been "trapped" in the Grand Canyon, we probably would not have given each other much of a second thought. God obviously had His hand in our meeting, however, even though at the time I didn't think so. For one thing, this lady was way too "religious" for me. And as for me, let's say I was not quite what she had in mind. I was not a Christian. I drank, a little too much at times. My language was, well, not always Godly. And I was divorced.

Crystal Rapid

96

But the Lord had scheduled enough time for us in this very magical place to get past those few "minor flaws" we both had. On the second night of our river trip, she started her ministry on my lost soul — not an easy project.

I vividly remember a very philosophical conversation about the meaning of life we had under the stars on the banks of the Colorado. My view was that the meaning of life was to have fun, while hers was to have a personal relationship with the Lord. During our nine days together, she continued to gently share the Gospel, enough to get me thinking.

Remember, I was immersed in evolutionary thought, which, contrary to what you might have been told by evolutionists themselves, seeks to eliminate God from all reality. The logical extension of this – that we are not responsible to anyone, that there are no absolute truths in life, that we set our own rules and this life is all there is – was the backdrop for my lifestyle.

My life as a guide consisted of telling folks that the exquisite and varied rock layers in the Grand Canyon came about through completely natural processes, even though, deep in my heart, I had lots of questions about how these processes could have created what we see today. I knew about the biblical story of Noah's flood, but it was just that…a story.

After the trip, the lady, who read her Bible and believed it, sent me a Bible which traveled halfway around the world with me on a trip

Tom explains the Great Unconformity in Blacktail Canyon.
(Keith Swenson)

to the Himalayas in Pakistan. My worldview began to be transformed slowly as I read the Word of God in my little tent at 12,500 feet in near-zero degree weather. I distinctly remember reading by headlamp as the cold invaded my small space. I spent hours reading and often lit a small candle to add just a little warmth to my den. Time after time I picked the Bible up, read it, put it down, and mulled over what truth might be in its pages. Was this God of the Bible real?

My eyes kept falling on a prayer this lady had written in my Bible:

Dear Lord,
I know I have done wrong,
that I miss the mark of perfection.
I am willing to turn from my sins.
I believe Jesus Christ died for me.
Please come into my life and forgive me.
I receive You in my life as my Lord and Savior,
as best I know right now.

Tom's Story

I read this prayer tens of times before it really started to sink in. And at some point, I started to mean it. In October 1994, I returned from Pakistan a child of Christ. I had made a conscious decision to believe in the Gospel, and to accept Christ as my Lord and Savior.

You likely have no idea how this choice impacted not only my heart, but my head as well. The uniformitarian view of life, the belief that what we see is the product of billions of years of gradual change, doesn't jibe with the biblical account of origins. From warm moonlit nights in the Canyon, to my encounter with the Deity in the Himalayan cold, to endless reflection on the meaning of it all, I began to see life in a much different way.

The way I saw the Canyon — this place that I love and that draws me back year after year — was changing in the most profound way as well. Some would say the change was just plain ridiculous.

For 15 years I taught the evolutionary model of how the Canyon was formed, but it never really made complete sense. There were too many totally unbelievable things that had to happen for this model to work. Genesis tells an altogether different story. When I studied the creation model, things started to come together. The creation model makes a lot more sense, is much easier to believe, and answers more questions than the million-of-years, molecule-to-man theories. I came to believe that it takes more "faith" to believe in evolution than in creation.

Understand that very few Grand Canyon guides include the Bible in their required gear for a trip. And most of them don't quote Genesis while floating through the Granite Gorge with walls towering more than a mile above them. It doesn't fit today's widely

98

"Let's go boatin'!" (Courtesy of Arizona River Runners)

accepted model. More than that, to publicly give a nod to the validity of Genesis is to invite criticism.

Yet, like the apostle James, I count it all joy. My new understanding of my surroundings has been incredibly freeing. Even the Canyon has taken on a more beautiful look. Life makes more sense to me now — this life and the life to come.

I hope you'll come to believe, as I do, that the Grand Canyon is not only a chilling museum of death, with its trillions of fossilized creatures who were terrorized as walls of mud and water froze them in time. It is also a reminder to Christians that God's Word is true and can be relied upon. And if the Flood happened, as Genesis clearly says it did, then the Judge of Genesis is also coming as the Redeemer so gloriously revealed in the last book of the Bible — the book of Revelation.

I know a little about geology and other fields of science which are so gripped by the evolutionary philosophies of today. I also know a little about men's hearts. The Grand Canyon is a symbol of sin and what it once caused. That's the fundamental truth that is found there. This profound truth humbles me, as I am always humbled when the water carries me forward on another trip through God's gargantuan cathedral. And as you travel the Canyon you can see it, the Canyon, reaching out to the hearts of those passing through. It can truly be a life — and heart — changing experience.

If you would like to put your trust in the Lord and learn how to develop a personal relationship with Jesus Christ, you can begin by praying the prayer on page 97, the one that lady wrote in my Bible. Then seek out a church that believes in and teaches that the Bible is the inerrant Word of God! Find a church where you can experience the four "F's." That is a church where you will be "**F**ed" the truth, directly from the Bible, not someone's opinion. It should be a church where you "**F**it in," where you can enjoy the "**F**ellowship" of other believers, and, where you will be "**F**ruitful" in your new walk with the Lord. This is a life-changing commitment that will not only determine where you will spend eternity, but will change the way you view life, and the Grand Canyon.

Oh yes, "that lady." Well, she was right — the true meaning of life is to have a personal relationship with the one true and living God. But she, on the other hand, was a little longer project than my seeing the truth. It took me about a year to get her to say, "Yes!" Her name is Paula and we were married the following October, on the day the Lord had planned all along. I dedicate this book to her for the Light she brought into my life.

In 1997, Paula and I started Canyon Ministries, which is our way of sharing the majesty of the Grand Canyon from a biblical world view. We encourage people to put on their biblical "Son glasses" and help equip them to uphold the authority of Scripture from the very first verse.

So, come join us and see His handiwork for yourself — and ***"Let's go boatin'!"***

TOM VAIL

Steven Austin, Ph.D. Geology — He has a B.S. from the University of Washington, M.S. from San Jose State University and Ph.D. from the Pennsylvania State University, all in geology. His professional memberships include the Geological Society of America, the American Association of Petroleum Geologists, the Society for Sedimentary Geology, the International Association of Sedimentologists.

John Baumgardner, Ph.D. Geophysics and Space Physics — He has a B.S. in electrical engineering from Texas Tech University, an M.S. in electrical engineering from Princeton University and an M.S. and Ph.D. in geophysics and space physics from UCLA. Dr. Baumgardner has served as staff scientist in the Fluid Dynamics Group of the Theoretical Division at Los Alamos National Laboratory in New Mexico since 1984. He is well-known for his development of the TERRA program, a 3-D spherical finite element model for the earth's mantle.

Ken Cumming, Ph.D. Biology — He has a B.S. in biology/chemistry with honors from Tufts University, a master's in biology from Harvard, and the Ph.D. in biology with a major in ecology and a minor in biochemistry from Harvard University. He has been on the faculties at the Virginia Polytechnic Institute and State University (Virginia Tech), the University of Wisconsin at La Crosse, and Western Wisconsin Technological Institute at La Crosse.

Duane Gish, Ph.D. Biochemistry — He has a B.S. in chemistry from UCLA and a Ph.D. in biochemistry from the University of California (Berkeley). He spent a total of 18 years in biochemical research; with Cornell University Medical College (NYC), with the Virus Laboratory, University of California-Berkley, and on the research staff of the Upjohn Pharmaceutical Company. He has published approximately 40 articles in scientific journals.

Werner Gitt, Ph. D. Engineering, Germany — Dr. Gitt is one of the world's most active scientists engaged in original research and writing. A director and professor of the German Federal Institute of Physics, he received his doctorate (*summa cum laude*) from the Technical University of Aachen, Germany, in 1970. On the way to receiving his doctorate, he won that university's prestigious Borchers Medal. For more than 15 years he has also been a regular guest lecturer at the State Independent Theological University of Basel, Switzerland, on the subject of "the Bible and science."

Ken Ham — He is the executive director of the Bible-defending ministry *Answers in Genesis*. Ken Ham is one of the most in-demand Christian speakers in North America. Ham — a native Australian now residing near Cincinnati — is the author of numerous books on Genesis, dinosaurs, and the evil fruits of evolutionary thinking, including a book on the origin of "races" and racism, *One Blood*. In addition to a very heavy speaking load, Ken hosts the daily radio program *Answers*, now heard on 260 stations in America and 40 overseas.

Bill Hoesch, M.S. Geology — He has a B.A. in geology from the University of Colorado and an M.S. in geology from the ICR Graduate School. For several years Bill was employed in petroleum exploration and has extensive international experience including teaching geology in China. Bill then returned to the United States where he took a position as Public Information Officer at ICR, and then Research Geologist, where he currently assists in mineral isolation of RATE project rocks, and field work in parts of Arizona, Nevada, and Utah on a stratigraphic study of a nautiloid mass-kill deposit.

Russ Humphreys, Ph.D. Physics — He has a B.S. in physics from Duke University and a Ph.D. in physics from Louisiana State University. He has worked for Sandia National Laboratories since 1979 in nuclear physics, geophysics, pulsed power research, theoretical atomic and nuclear physics, and the Particle Beam Fusion Project. He was co-inventor of special laser-triggered "Rimfire" high-voltage switches.

Alex Lalomov, Ph.D. Geology, Russia — He has an M.S. in geochemistry from Leningrad State University and a Ph.D. in submarine geology from the USSR National Research Institute of Ocean Geology. Dr. Lalomov is a member of the Society of the Geological Society of USSR (Russia since 1992), the Geographical Society of Russia, and the Ecology Union of Russia.

John MacArthur, Th.M Theology — He completed seminary training at Talbot Theological Seminary and is pastor-teacher of Grace Community Church in Sun Valley, California, and president of The Master's College and Seminary. The author of numerous best-selling books, his popular expository style of teaching can be heard daily on his internationally syndicated radio broadcast "Grace to You." He edited the MacArthur Study Bible, which won the Gold Medallion Award. (Dr. MacArthur's contribution for this book was excerpted from a sermon, and is used by permission.)

Saddle Falls (Chuck Hill)

Henry M. Morris, Ph.D. Hydraulic Engineering — He has a B.S. from Rice University with honors in civil engineering and M.S. and Ph.D. degrees from the University of Minnesota. Dr. Morris majored in engineering hydraulics/hydrology while minoring in geology and mathematics. From 1957 to 1970 he was head of the Department of Civil Engineering at the Virginia Polytechnic Institute and State University (Virginia Tech).

John Morris, Ph.D. Geological Engineering — He has a B.S. in civil engineering from Virginia Polytechnic Institute and an M.S. and Ph.D. in geological engineering from the University of Oklahoma. He was a research assistant from 1978–1980 and assistant professor of geological engineering from 1980–1984 at Oklahoma University as well.

Terry Mortenson, Ph.D. History of Geology — He studied math and was led to Christ at the University of Minnesota. In 1975 he joined the staff of Campus Crusade for Christ and ministered to college students, first in the USA for four years and then for nearly two decades in eastern Europe. He earned an M.Div from Trinity Evangelical Divinity School in Chicago and a Ph.D. in history of geology from Coventry University in England. In 2001 he became a speaker, researcher, and writer for Answers in Genesis in Kentucky.

Mike Oard, M.S. Atmospheric Science — He has a B.S. and M.S. in atmospheric science from the University of Washington. He was a research assistant at the University of Washington for five years. He was a meteorologist with the National Weather Service, Great Falls, Montana, for over 27 years and lead forecaster for 20 years. Mr. Oard was published in the *Journal of Meteorology* among others.

Gary Parker, Ed.D. Biology — He has a B.A. in biology/chemistry(high honors) from Wabash College, Crawfordville, IN, an M.S. in biology/physiology, and an Ed.D. in biology with a cognate in paleontology from Ball State University. He has published a number of books from both a secular and creation point of view.

Scott Rugg, M.S. Geology — He is a licensed consulting engineering geologist and president of Rugg Geosciences, Inc. Mr. Rugg received a bachelor's of science degree in geology from San Diego State University in 1982 and a master's of science in geology from the Institute for Creation Research (ICR) in 1986. He has worked in the field of geotechnical engineering for over 17 years and has been involved with several thousand projects throughout the state of California. He has participated as a guide on numerous ICR- sponsored Grand Canyon and Mount St. Helens trips and has taught geology courses at both Christian Heritage College and ICR. Other contributions include several professional presentations at the International Conference of Creationism and work with several ICR scientists on a variety of research projects.

Andrew Snelling, Ph.D. Geology, Australia — He has a B.Sc. with first class honors in applied geology from the University of New South Wales in Sydney, Australia and a Ph.D. in geology from the University of Sydney. He worked for a number of years in the mining industry in locations throughout Australia undertaking mineral exploration surveys and field research. He has also been a consultant research geologist for more than a decade to the Australian Nuclear Science and Technology Organization and the U.S. Nuclear Regulatory Commission for internationally funded research on the geology and geochemistry of uranium ore deposits as analogues of nuclear waste disposal sites.

Dr. Keith Swenson, M.D. — He has a B.S. in zoology and pre-medical studies from the University of Idaho and an M.D. from Washington University School of Medicine (St. Louis, Missouri). He is a diplomate of the American Board of Internal Medicine and the American Board of Dermatology. Dr. Swenson has served as a clinical assistant professor of Dermatology (University of Illinois) and has practiced clinical medicine for over 20 years.

Larry Vardiman, Ph.D. Atmospheric Science — He has a B.S. in physics from the University of Missouri at Rolla, a B.S. in meteorology from St. Louis University and an M.S. and Ph.D. in atmospheric science from Colorado State University. Dr. Vardiman is a member of the American Meteorological Society.

Tas Walker, Ph.D. Mechanical Engineering, Australia — He has a bachelor of engineering with first class honors and a doctorate in mechanical engineering. He has been involved in the planning, design, and operation of power stations for over 20 years with the electricity industry in Queensland, Australia. Recently, Dr. Walker returned to university study, and completed a bachelor of science, majoring in earth science, followed by First Class Honours in 1998. He has also set up an internet site (www.uq.net.au/~zztbwalk/) about geology and the Bible. The site describes the basis of this model and a practical application to the Great Artesian Basin of Australia.

John Whitcomb, Th.M Theology — He graduated with honors from Princeton University in 1948, with a B.A. degree in ancient and European history. He then graduated from Grace Theological Seminary in Winona Lake, Indiana, with B.D. and Th.M degrees. He served as professor of theology and Old Testament at Grace Theological Seminary for 38 years. Dr. Whitcomb lived in China for 3 years and later served his country in Europe during WW II. In 1961, Dr. Whitcomb co-authored (with Henry Morris) the landmark book *The Genesis Flood*, which ushered-in renewed interest in creationism.

Dr. Carl Wieland, M.D., Australia — He is in great demand worldwide as a speaker on the evidence for creation and the Flood. Based in Australia, Dr. Wieland is the founder and editor of the full-color family *Creation* magazine.

Kurt Wise, Ph.D. Geology (Paleontology) — He has a B.A. in geophysical sciences from the University of Chicago, and an M.A. and Ph.D. in geology (paleontology) from Harvard University, where Stephen J. Gould was his principal advisor. Dr. Wise is currently Director of Origins Research and Associate Professor of Science, Division of Mathematics and Natural Science, Bryan College, Dayton, Tennessee.

The Lord is my rock and my fortress . .
. — Psalm 18:2

All of the materials listed here were authored from a biblical world view. They do, however, represent a range of theories within that world view.

BOOKS

Austin, Steve. *Grand Canyon: Monument to Catastrophe.* El Cajon, CA: ICR, 1993.

Brand, Leonard. *Faith, Reason, and Earth History.* Berrien Springs, MI: Andrews University Press, 1997.

Gish, Duane. *Evolution, The Fossils STILL Say No!* Green Forest, AR: Master Books, 1995.

Gitt, Werner. *If Animals Could Talk.* Green Forest, AR: Master Books, 2001.

Ham, Ken. *The New Answers Book:* Green Forest, AR: Master Books, 2006.

Ham, Ken. *Evolution: The Lie.* Green Forest, AR: Master Books, 1987.

Ham, Ken. *Why Won't They Listen?* Green Forest, AR: Master Books, 2002.

Humphreys, Russell. *Starlight and Time.* Green Forest, AR: Master Books, 1994.

Morris, Henry; Whitcomb, John. **The Genesis Flood.* Winona Lake, IN: BMH Books, 1979. *Editor's note: this classic work, which launched the modern creationist revolution, first appeared in 1961 and therefore some of the geological material in this book may be considered outdated. But the overall framework remains foundational in the thinking of creationist scientists worldwide.

Morris, Henry. *The Genesis Record.* Grand Rapids, MI: Baker Books, 1976.

Morris, Henry; Parker, Gary. *What is Creation Science?* Green Forest, AR: Master Books, 1982.

Morris, John. *The Geology Book.* Green Forest, AR: Master Books, 2000.

Morris, John. *The Young Earth.* Green Forest, AR: Master Books, 1994.

Palmer, Trevor. *Controversy, Catastrophism and Evolution: the Ongoing Debate.* New York, NY: Plenum Publishing Corp., 1999.

Parker, Gary. *Creation: Facts of Life.* Green Forest, AR: Master Books, 1994.

Parker, Gary. *Dry Bones…and Other Fossils.* Green Forest, AR: Master Books, 1997.

Roth, Ariel. Origins: *Linking Science and Scripture.* Hagerstown, MD: Review & Herald Publishing Assn., 1998.

Rudwick, M.J.S. *The Meaning of Fossils: Episodes in the History of Paleontology.* New York, NY: Elsevier Science, 1972.

Vail, Tom; Oard, Mike; Hergenrather, John; Bokovoy, Dennis. *True North Series: Your Guide to the Grand Canyon.* Green Forest, AR: Master Books, 2008

Vardiman, Larry. *Over the Edge.* Green Forest, AR: Master Books, 1999.

Vardiman, Snelling, and Chaffin, editors. *Radioisotopes and the Age of the Earth: A Young-Earth Creationist Research Initiative.* El Cajon, CA, ICR, 2001.

Whitcomb, John. *The World That Perished.* Winona Lake, IN: BMH Books, 1979.

TECHNICAL PAPERS

"British Scriptural Geologists in the First Half of the Nineteenth Century," Parts 1-8, *Technical Journal*, volumes 11:2; 11:3; 12:2; 12:3; 13:1; 14:1; 16:2; 16:3. www.answersingenesis.org

VIDEOS

Grand Canyon Catastrophe, ICR, 1996
The Bible and Science, 12 video set, Whitcomb

WEB SITES

Answers in Genesis — www.AnswersinGenesis.org
Canyon Ministries — www.CanyonMinistries.com
Institute for Creation Research — www.ICR.org
Dr. John Whitcomb — www.whitcombministries.org

Shoshone Point, viewed from the South Rim

Tom, Canyon Ministries and Grand Canyon boatman

Charly, chief photographer and Grand Canyon boatman

Born in southern California, Tom Vail was managing the corporate computer center for a Fortune 500 company in downtown Los Angeles when he went on vacation in 1980 – a vacation that truly turned into the adventure of a lifetime. It was a rafting trip through the Grand Canyon with Georgie's Royal River Rats, run by Georgie Clark, one of the original pioneers of rafting the Canyon. One of the regular boatmen didn't show up, and, with no prior experience, Tom was "drafted" to help row a boat through the Canyon. By the end of the trip he was hooked, and two years later he left the corporate life to become a career rafting guide. He worked with Georgie for 12 years, joining Arizona River Runners after her death.

Tom also worked part-time for the Grand Canyon National Park Service, running VIP and research trips, and is a past elected member of the board of directors for Grand Canyon River Guides. Tom and his wife, Paula, live in Phoenix, Arizona, and run Canyon Ministries, which offers Christ-centered rafting trips through the Grand Canyon. Besides their own trips, they run the Grand Canyon rafting tours for both Answers in Genesis (AiG) and Institute for Creation Research (ICR).

Through his ministry work in the Canyon, Tom has had the opportunity to spend time with many of the contributors to this book. His love for the Lord Jesus Christ and his heart for sharing the creation message has put him in a unique position in the Grand Canyon guiding community. If you are interested in information about Canyon Ministries, visit their website at: www.CanyonMinistries.com.

View upstream above Granite Narrows

Charly Heavenrich's passion is sharing "the Canyon Experience" with people in a way that has meaning and value for them. He has done this since 1978, not only as a Grand Canyon rafting guide but also as a speaker, taking audiences on a vicarious journey through the Grand Canyon. He is the author of *Dancing on the Edge*, an inspiring journey through the Grand Canyon, and is a personal and professional coach. Although he does not share the creationist point of view, he is profoundly moved by the Canyon and the depth of courage and ability he sees in the people who travel with him. His river-level images provide a seldom seen view of the majesty of the Grand Canyon. Charly lives in Boulder, Colorado, and is committed to sharing the possibilities and adventure of life. For information about his speaking programs, books, and custom prints, visit his website at: www.charlyheavenrich.com.